GRADE

3

ReadyGEN™

Text Collection

PEARSON

Glenview, Illinois • Boston, Massachusetts • Chandler, Arizona • Upper Saddle River, New Jersey

ISBN-13: 978-0-328-78844-6
ISBN-10: 0-328-78844-9
1 2 3 4 5 6 7 8 9 10 V003 17 16 15 14 13

Table of Contents

Unit 1 Observing the World Around Us

Unit 2 Connecting Character, Culture, and Community

Thunder Cake

PATRICIA POLACCO

On sultry summer days at my grandma's farm in Michigan, the air gets damp and heavy. Stormclouds drift low over the fields. Birds fly close to the ground. The clouds glow for an instant with a sharp, crackling light, and then a roaring, low, tumbling sound of thunder makes the windows shudder in their panes. The sound used to scare me when I was little. I loved to go to Grandma's house (Babushka, as I used to call my grandma, had come from Russia years before), but I feared Michigan's summer storms. I feared the sound of thunder more than anything. I always hid under the bed when the storm moved near the farmhouse.

This is the story of how my grandma—my Babushka—helped me overcome my fear of thunderstorms.

Grandma looked at the horizon, drew a deep breath and said, "This is Thunder Cake baking weather, all right. Looks like a storm coming to me."

“Child, you come out
from under that bed.
It’s only thunder you’re
hearing,” my grandma said.

The air was hot, heavy
and damp. A loud clap of
thunder shook the house,
rattled the windows and
made me grab her close.

“Steady, child, she cooed.
“Unless you let go of me,
we won’t be able to make a
Thunder Cake today!”

"Thunder Cake?" I stammered as I hugged her even closer.

"Don't pay attention to that old thunder, except to see how close the storm is getting. When you see the lightning, start counting…real slow. When you hear the thunder, stop counting. That number is how many miles away the storm is. Understand?" she asked. "We need to know how far away the storm is, so we have time to make the cake and get it into the oven before the storm comes, or it won't be real Thunder Cake."

Her eyes surveyed the black clouds a way off in the distance. Then she strode into the kitchen. Her worn hands pulled a thick book from the shelf above the woodstove.

"Let's find that recipe, child," she crowed as she lovingly fingered the grease-stained pages to a creased spot.

"Here it is…Thunder Cake!"

She carefully penned the ingredients on a piece of notepaper. " Now let's gather all the things we'll need!" she exclaimed as she scurried toward the back door.

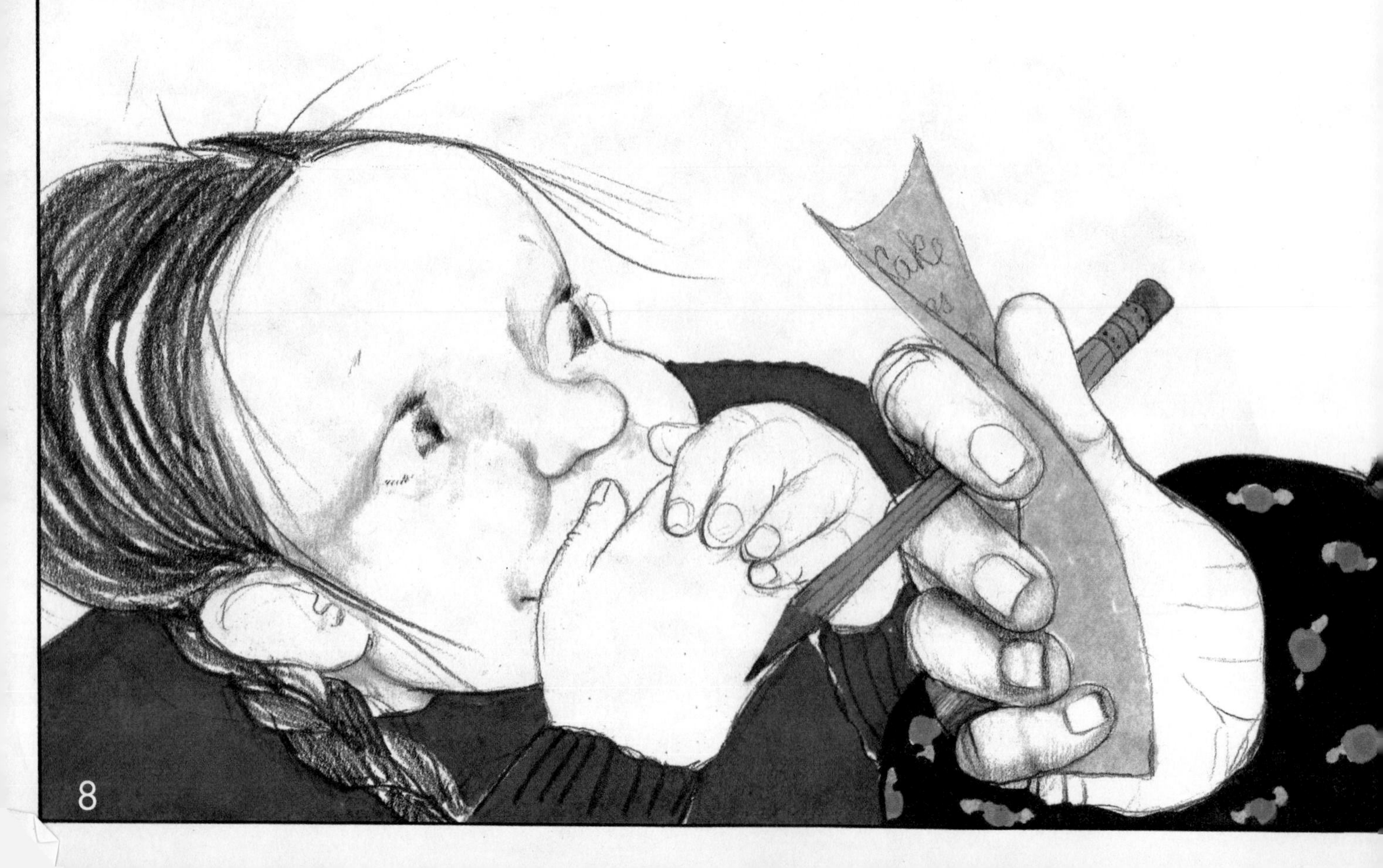

We were by the barn door when a huge bolt of lightning flashed. I started counting, like grandma told me to, "1-2-3-4-5-6-7-8-9-10."

Then the thunder ROARED!

"Ten miles… it's ten miles away," Grandma said as she looked at the sky. "About an hour away, I'd say. You'll have to hurry, child. Gather them eggs careful-like," she said

Eggs from mean old Nellie Peck Hen. I was scared. I knew she would try to peck me.

"I'm here, she won't hurt you. Just get them eggs," Grandma said softly.

The lightning flashed again. "1-2-3-4-5-6-7-8-9" I counted.

"Nine miles," Grandma reminded me.

Milk was next. Milk from old Kick Cow. As Grandma milked her, Kick Cow turned and looked mean, right at me. I was scared. She looked so big.

Zip went the lightning. "1-2-3-4-5-6-7-8," I counted. BAROOOOOOOOM went the thunder.

"Eight miles, child," Grandma croaked. "Now we have to get chocolate and sugar and flour from the dry shed."

I was scared as we walked down the path from the farmhouse through Tangleweed Woods to the dry shed. Suddenly the lightning slit the sky!

"1-2-3-4-5-6-7" I counted. BOOOOOOM BA-BOOOOOOM, crashed the thunder. It scared me a lot, but I kept walking with Grandma.

Another jagged edge of lightning flashed as I crept into the dry shed! "1-2-3-4-5-6" I counted.

CRACKLE, CRACKLE BOOOOOOOM, KA-BOOOOOM, the thunder bellowed. It was dark and I was scared.

"I'm here, child," Grandma said softly from the doorway. "Hurry now, we haven't got much time. We've got everything but the secret ingredient."

"Three overripe tomatoes and some strawberries," Grandma whispered as she squinted at the list.

I climbed up high on the trellis. The ground looked a long way down. I was scared.

"I'm here, child," she said. Her voice was steady and soft. "You won't fall."

I reached three luscious tomatoes while she picked strawberries. Lightning again!

"1-2-3-4-5" I counted.

KA-BANG BOOOOOOOOAROOOOM, the thunder growled.

We hurried back to the house and the warm kitchen, and we measured the ingredients. I poured them into the mixing bowl while Grandma mixed. I churned butter for the frosting and melted chocolate. Finally, we poured the batter into the cake pans and put them into the oven together.

Lightning lit the kitchen! I only counted to three and the thunder RRRRUMBLED and CRASHED.

"Three miles away," Grandma said, "and the cake is in the oven. We made it! We'll have a real Thunder Cake!"

As we waited for the cake, Grandma looked out the window for a long time. "Why, you aren't afraid of thunder. You're too brave!" she said as she looked right at me.

"I'm not brave, Grandma," I said. "I was under the bed! Remember?"

"But you got out from under it," she answered, "and you got eggs from mean old Nellie Peck Hen, you got milk from old Kick Cow, you went through Tangleweed Woods to the dry shed, you climbed the trellis in the barnyard. From where I sit, only a very brave person could have done all them things!"

I thought and thought as the storm rumbled closer. She was right. I was brave!

"Brave people can't be afraid of a sound, child," she said as we spread out the tablecloth and set the table. When we were done, we hurried into the kitchen to take the cake out of the oven. After the cake had cooled, we frosted it.

Just then the lightning flashed, and this time it lit the whole sky. Even before the last flash had faded, the thunder ROLLED, BOOOOOMED, CRASHED, and BBBBAAAAARRRRROOOOOOOOMMMMMMMMMMED just above us. The storm was here!

"Perfect," Grandma cooed, "just perfect." She beamed as she added the last strawberry to the glistening chocolate frosting on top of our Thunder Cake.

As rain poured down on our roof, Grandma cut a wedge for each of us. She poured us steaming cups of tea from the samovar.

When the thunder ROARED above us so hard it shook the windows and rattled the dishes in the cupboards, we just smiled and ate our Thunder Cake.

From that time on, I never feared the voice of thunder again.

The Lemonade War

by Jacqueline Davies

Location, Location, Location

Evan Treski and his younger sister Jessie are in a contest to see who can earn $100 selling lemonade by Saturday. So far Jessie is winning!

Evan was in trouble. So far, he'd earned forty-seven dollars and eleven cents, which was more money than he'd ever had in his whole life. But today was Friday. There were only three days left. Three days to beat Jessie. He needed to earn almost fifty-three dollars to win the bet. And that meant each day he had to earn—

Evan tried to do the math in his head. Fifty-three divided by three. Fifty-three divided by three. His brain spun like a top. He didn't know where to begin.

He went to his desk, pulled out a piece of paper—his basketball schedule from last winter— and flipped it over to the back. He found the stub of a pencil in his bottom desk drawer, and on the paper he wrote

$$53 \div 3 =$$

He stared and stared at the equation on the page. The number fifty-three was just too big. He didn't know how to do it.

"Jessie would know how," he muttered, scribbling hard on the page. Jessie could do long division. Jessie had her multiplication facts memorized all the way up to fourteen times fourteen. Jessie would look at a problem like this and just do it in her head. *Snap*.

Evan felt his mouth getting tight, his fingers gripping the pencil too hard, as he scribbled a dark storm cloud on the page. His math papers from school were always covered in X's. Nobody else got as many X's as he did. Nobody.

Draw a picture. Mrs. DeFazio's voice floated in his head. She had always reminded him to draw a picture when he couldn't figure out how to start a math problem. *A picture of what?* he asked in his head. *Anything,* came the answer.

Anything? Yes, anything, as long as there are fifty-three of them.

Dollar signs. Evan decided to draw dollar signs. He started to draw three rows of dollar signs. "One, two, three," he counted, as he drew:

"Four, five, six." He drew:

By the time he reached fifty-three, his page looked like this:

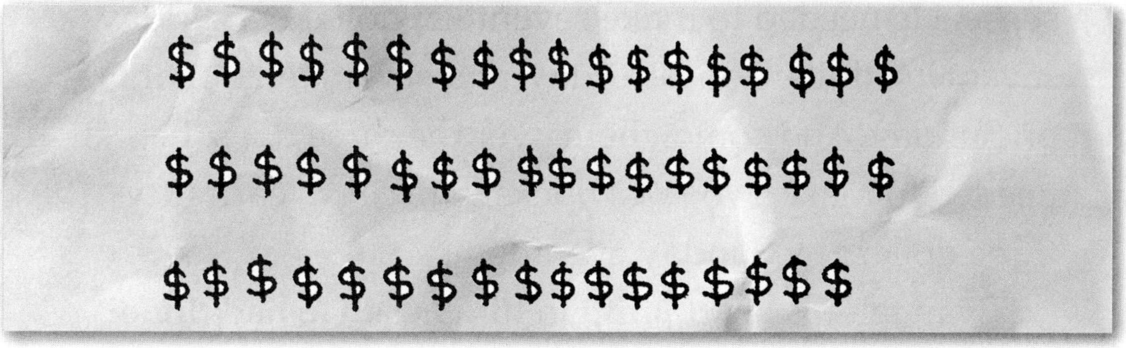

There were seventeen dollar signs in each row. And then those two extra dollar signs left over. Evan drew a ring around those two extras.

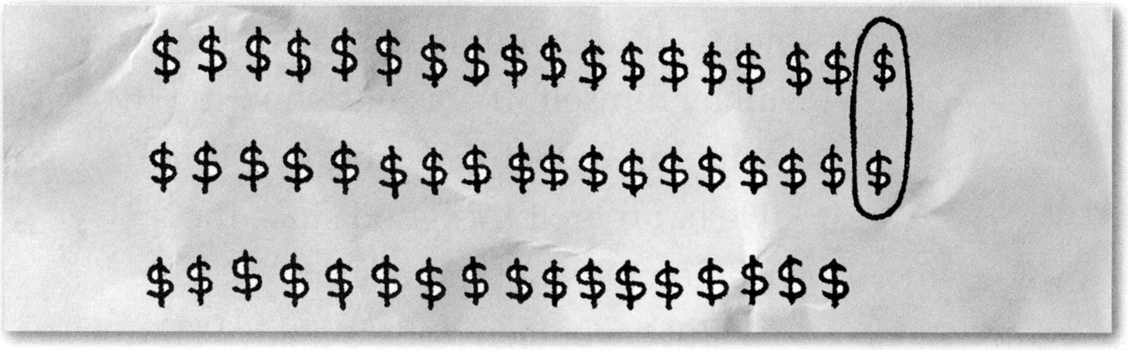

Seventeen dollar signs. And two left over. Evan stared at the picture for a long time. He wrote "Friday" next to the first row, "Saturday" next to the second row, and "Sunday" next to the third row.

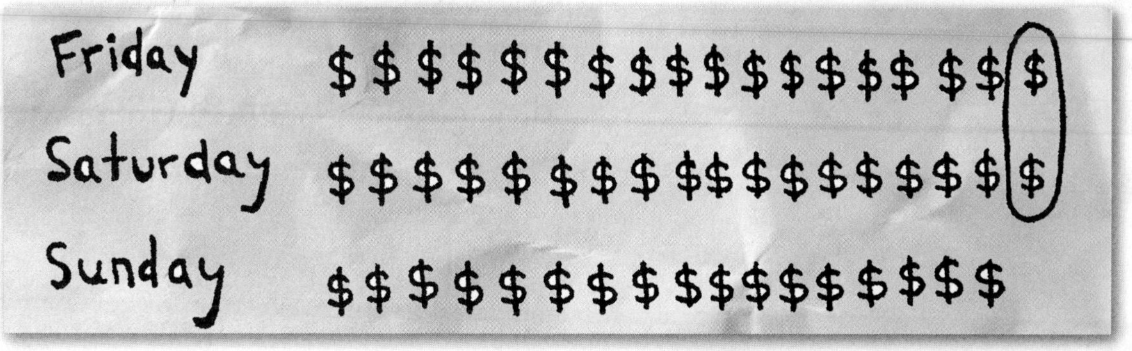

Evan looked at the picture. It started to make sense. He needed to make seventeen dollars on Friday, seventeen dollars on Saturday, and seventeen dollars on Sunday. And somewhere over the three days, he needed to make two *extra* bucks in order to earn fifty-three dollars by Sunday evening.

Evan felt his heart jump in his chest. He had done it. He had figured out fifty-three divided by three. That was a *fourth-grade* problem. That was *fourth-grade* math. And he hadn't even started fourth-grade! And no one had helped him. Not Mom, not Grandma, not Jessie. He'd done it all by himself. It was like shooting the winning basket in double overtime! He hadn't felt this good since the Lemonade War had begun.

But seventeen dollars a day? How was he going to do that? Yesterday he'd made forty-five dollars, but that was because he'd had help (and free supplies) from his friends. They weren't going to want to run a lemonade stand every day. Especially on the last days of summer vacation.

He needed a plan. Something that would guarantee good sales. The weather was holding out, that was for sure. It was going to hit 95 degrees today. A real scorcher. People would be thirsty, all right. Evan closed his eyes and imagined a crowd of thirsty people, all waving dollar bills at him. Now where was he going to find a lot of thirsty people with money to spend?

An idea popped into Evan's head. *Yep!* It was perfect. He just needed to find something with wheels to get him there.

It took Evan half an hour to drag his loaded wagon to the town center—a distance he usually traveled in less than five minutes by bike. But once he was there, he knew it was worth it.

It was lunchtime and the shaded benches on the town green were filled with people sprawling in the heat. Workers from the nearby stores on their half-hour lunch breaks, moms out with their kids, old people who didn't want to be cooped up in their houses all day. High school kids on skateboards slooshed by. Preschoolers climbed on the life-size sculpture of a circle of children playing ring-around-the-rosey. Dogs lay under trees, their tongues hanging out, *pant, pant, pant.*

Evan surveyed the scene and picked his spot, right in the center of the green where all the paths met. Anyone walking across the green would have to pass his stand. And who could resist lemonade on a day as hot as this?

But first he wheeled his wagon off to the side, parking it halfway under a huge rhododendron. Then he crossed the street and walked into the Big Dipper.

The frozen air felt good on his skin. It was like getting dunked in a vat of just-melted ice cream. And the smells—*mmmmmm*. A mix of vanilla, chocolate, coconut, caramel, and bubblegum. He looked at the tubs of ice cream, all in a row, carefully protected behind a pane of glass. The money in his pocket tingled. He had plenty left over after buying five cans of frozen lemonade mix with his earnings from yesterday. What would it hurt to buy just one cone? Or a milk shake? Or maybe both?

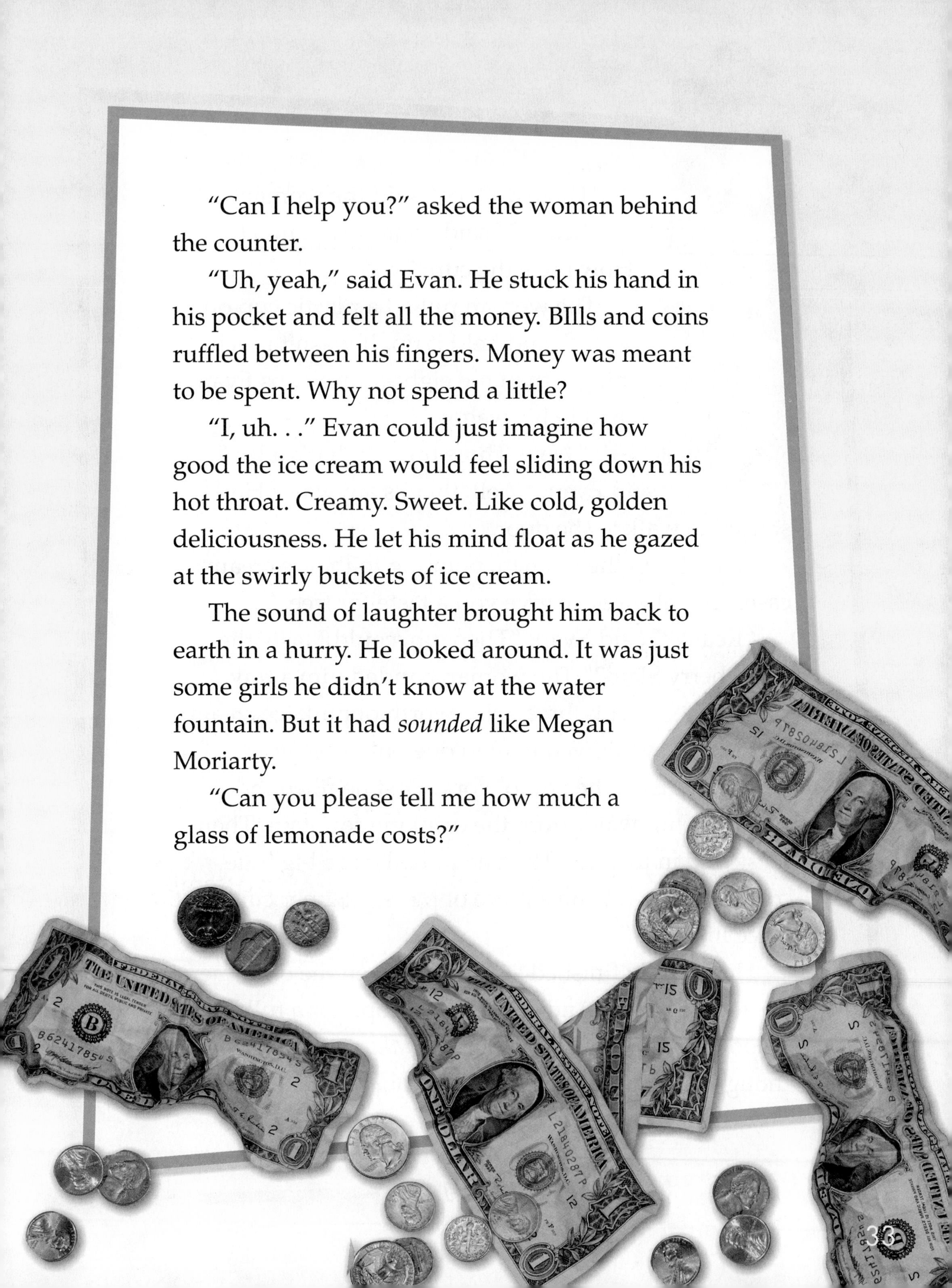

"Can I help you?" asked the woman behind the counter.

"Uh, yeah," said Evan. He stuck his hand in his pocket and felt all the money. BIlls and coins ruffled between his fingers. Money was meant to be spent. Why not spend a little?

"I, uh. . ." Evan could just imagine how good the ice cream would feel sliding down his hot throat. Creamy. Sweet. Like cold, golden deliciousness. He let his mind float as he gazed at the swirly buckets of ice cream.

The sound of laughter brought him back to earth in a hurry. He looked around. It was just some girls he didn't know at the water fountain. But it had *sounded* like Megan Moriarty.

"Can you please tell me how much a glass of lemonade costs?"

"Three dollars," said the woman.

"Really?" said Evan. "That much? How big's the cup?"

The woman pulled a plastic cup off a stack and held it up. It wasn't much bigger than the eight-ounce cups Evan had in his wagon.

"Wow. Three bucks. That's a lot," said Evan. "Well, thanks anyway." He started to walk to the door.

"Hey," said the woman, pointing to the ice cream case. "I'm allowed to give you a taste for free."

"Really?" said Evan. "Then, uh, could I taste the Strawberry Slam?" The woman handed him a tiny plastic spoon with three licks' worth of pink ice cream on it. Evan swallowed it all in one gulp. *Aahhh.*

Back outside, he got to work. First he filled his pitchers with water from the drinking fountain. Then he stirred in the mix. Then he pulled out a big blue marker and wrote on a piece of paper, "$2 per cup. Best price in town."

He'd barely finished setting up when the customers started lining up. And they didn't stop. For a full hour, he poured lemonade. *The world is a thirsty place,* he thought as he nearly emptied his fourth pitcher of the day. *And I am the Lemonade King*.

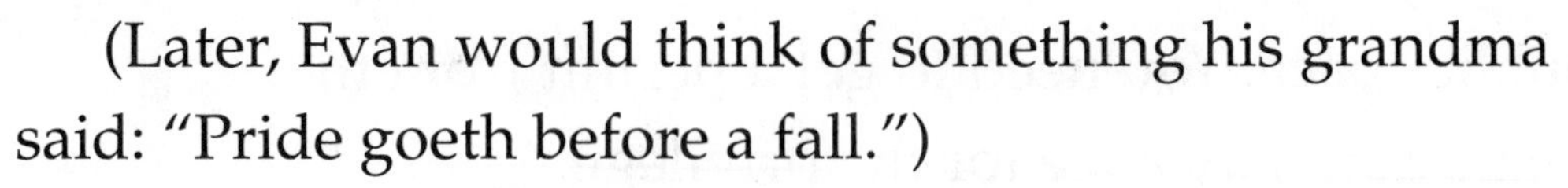

(Later, Evan would think of something his grandma said: "Pride goeth before a fall.")

When Evan looked up, there was Officer Ken, his hands on his hips, looking down on him. Evan gulped. He stared at the large holstered gun strapped to Officer Ken's belt.

"Hello," said Officer Ken, not smiling.

"Hi," said Evan. Officer Ken did the Bike Rodeo every year at Evan's school. He was also the cop who had shown up last fall when there was a hurt goose on the recess field. Officer Ken was always smiling. *Why isn't he smiling now?* Evan wondered.

"Do you have a permit?" asked Officer Ken. He had a very deep voice, even when he talked quietly, like he did now.

"You mean, like, a bike permit?" That's what the Rodeo was all about. If they passed the Rodeo, the third-graders got their bike permits, which meant they were allowed to ride to school.

"No. I mean a permit to sell food and beverages in a public space. You need to get a permit from the town hall. And pay a fee for the privilege."

Pay the town hall to run a lemonade stand? Was he kidding? Evan looked at Officer Ken's face. He didn't look like he was kidding.

"I didn't know I needed one," said Evan.

"Sorry, friend," said Officer Ken. "I'm going to have to shut you down. It's the law."

"But. . . but . . . there are lemonade stands all over town," said Evan. He thought of Jessie and Megan's lemonade stand. When he'd wheeled by with his wagon more than an hour ago, their stand had looked like a beehive, with small kids crowding around. He had read the sign over their stand: FREE FACE PAINTING! NAIL-POLISHING! HAIR- BRAIDING! What a gimmick! But it sure looked like it was working. "You know," said Evan, "there's a stand on Damon Road right now. You should go bust them."

Officer Ken smiled. "We tend to look the other way when it's in a residential neighborhood. But right here, on the town green, we have to enforce the law. Otherwise we'd have someone selling something every two feet."

"But---" There had to be some way to convince Officer Ken. How could Evan make him understand? "You see, I've got this little sister. And we've got a . . . a . . . competition going. To see who can sell the most lemonade. And I've *got* to win. Because she's . . . " He couldn't explain the rest. About fourth grade. And how embarrassed he was to be in the same class as his kid sister. And how it made him feel like a great big loser.

Evan looked up at Officer Ken. Officer Ken looked down at Evan. It was like Officer Ken was wearing a mask. A no-smiling, I'm-not-your-buddy mask.

Then Officer Ken shook his head and smiled and the mask feel off. " I've got a little sister, too," he said. "Love her to death, *now*, but when we were kids---" Officer Ken sucked in his breath and shook his head again. *"Hooo!"*

Then the mask came back, and Officer Ken looked right at Evan for ten very stern seconds.

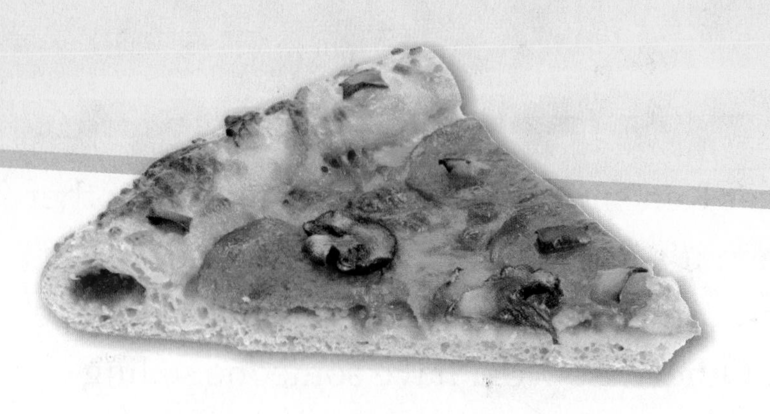

"Tell you what," said Officer Ken. " I *do* have to shut you down. The law's the law. But before I do, I'll buy one last glass of lemonade. How's that sound?"

Evan's face fell. "Sure," he said without enthusiasm. He poured an extra-tall cup and gave it to the policeman.

Officer Ken reached into his pocket and handed Evan a five-dollar bill. "Keep the change," he said. " A contribution to the Big Brother Fund. Now clean up your things and don't leave any litter behind." He lifted his cup in a toast as he walked away.

Evan watched him go. Wow, he thought. *I just sold the most expensive cup of lemonade in town.*

Evan stared at the five-dollar bill in his hand.

It was funny. Two days ago he would have felt as rich as a king to have that money in his hands. It was enough to buy two slices of pizza and a soda with his friends. It was enough to rent a video and have a late night at someone's house. It was enough to buy a whole bagful of his favorite candy mix at CVS.

Two days ago, he would have been jumping for joy.

Now he looked at the five dollars and thought, *It's nothing*. Compared to the one hundred dollars he needed to win the war, five dollars was *nothing*. He felt somehow that he's been robbed of something—maybe the happiness he should have been feeling.

He loaded everything from his stand into the wagon, making sure he didn't leave a scrap of litter behind. He still had a glassful of lemonade left in one pitcher, not to mention another whole pitcher already mixed up and unsold, so he poured himself a full cup. Then, before beginning the long, hot haul back to his house, he found an empty spot on a shaded bench and pulled his earnings out of his pockets.

He counted once. He counted twice. Very slowly.

He had made sixty-five dollars. The cups and lemonade mix had cost nine dollars. When he added in his earnings from Wednesday and Thursday, he had on hundred and three dollars and eleven cents. *Now* that's *enough,* he thought.

The MOON Seems to Change

by Franklyn M. Branley
illustrated by Barbara and Ed Emberley

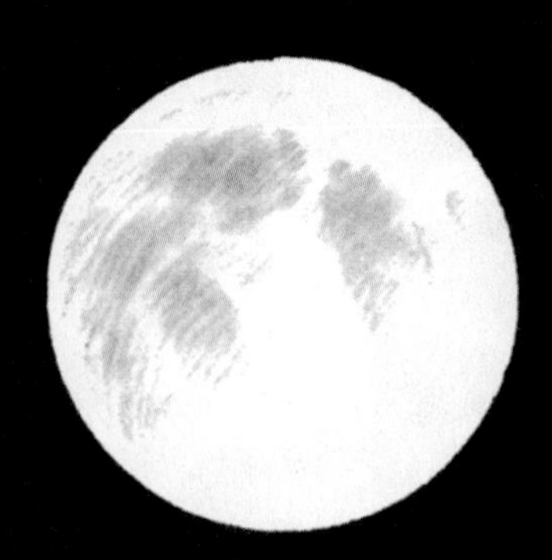

Tonight take a look at the sky. See if the moon is there.

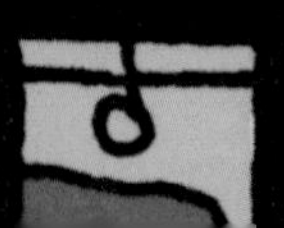

It may be big and round. It is a full moon.

FULL

Maybe you will see only part of it. It may be a quarter moon.

QUARTER

Or it may be only a little sliver. It is called a crescent moon.

CRESCENT

As the nights go by you can see changes in the moon. After the moon is full you see less and less of it. There are three or four nights with no moon at all. Then you see more and more of it. The moon seems to change

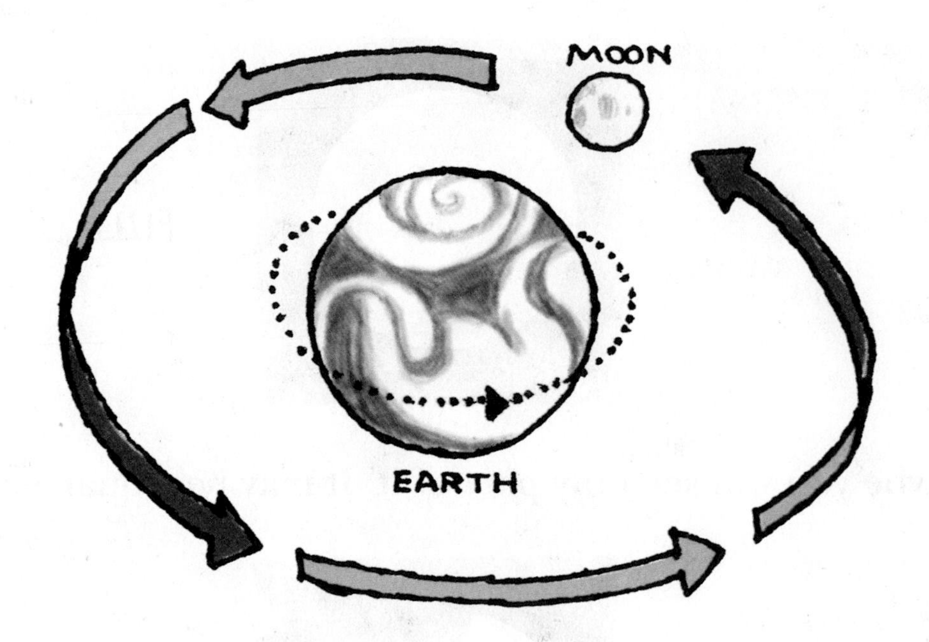

It really doesn't. It seems to change because the moon goes around Earth. As it goes around, we see more of it—the moon gets bigger. It is a waxing moon. Or we see less of it—the moon gets smaller. It is a waning moon.

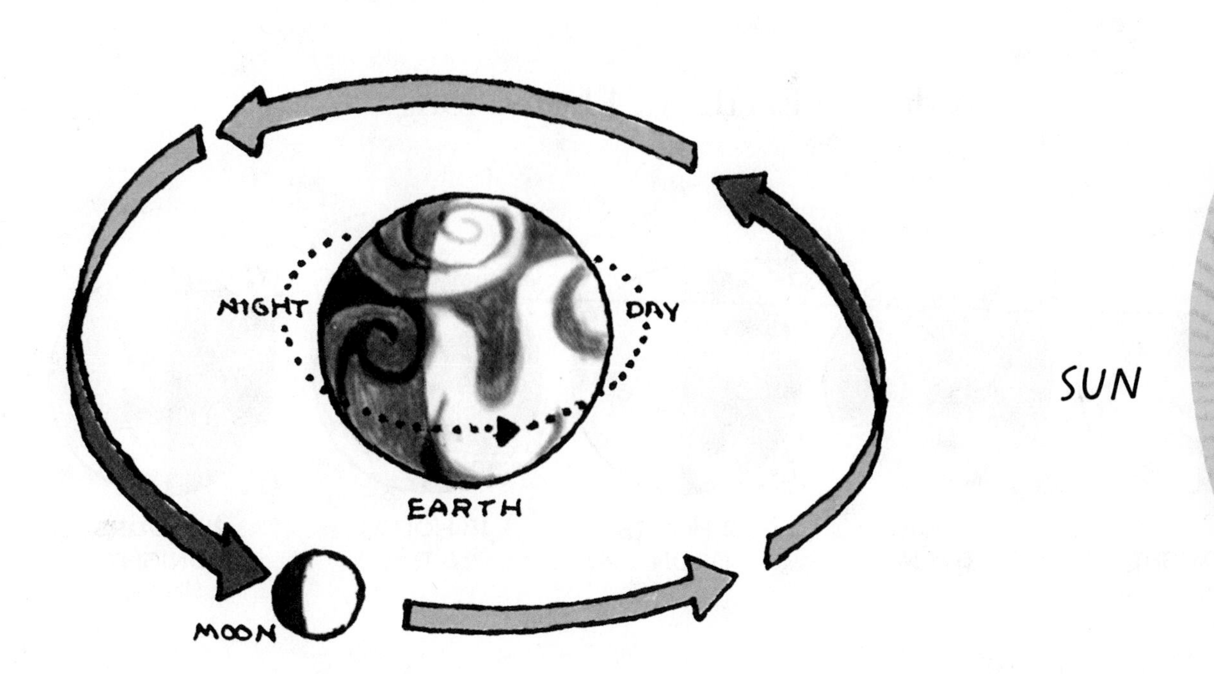

Half of the moon is always lighted by the sun. Half is lighted and half is always in darkness. It's the same with Earth. While one half of Earth is having sunshine and daylight, the other half is getting no sunshine. It is night.

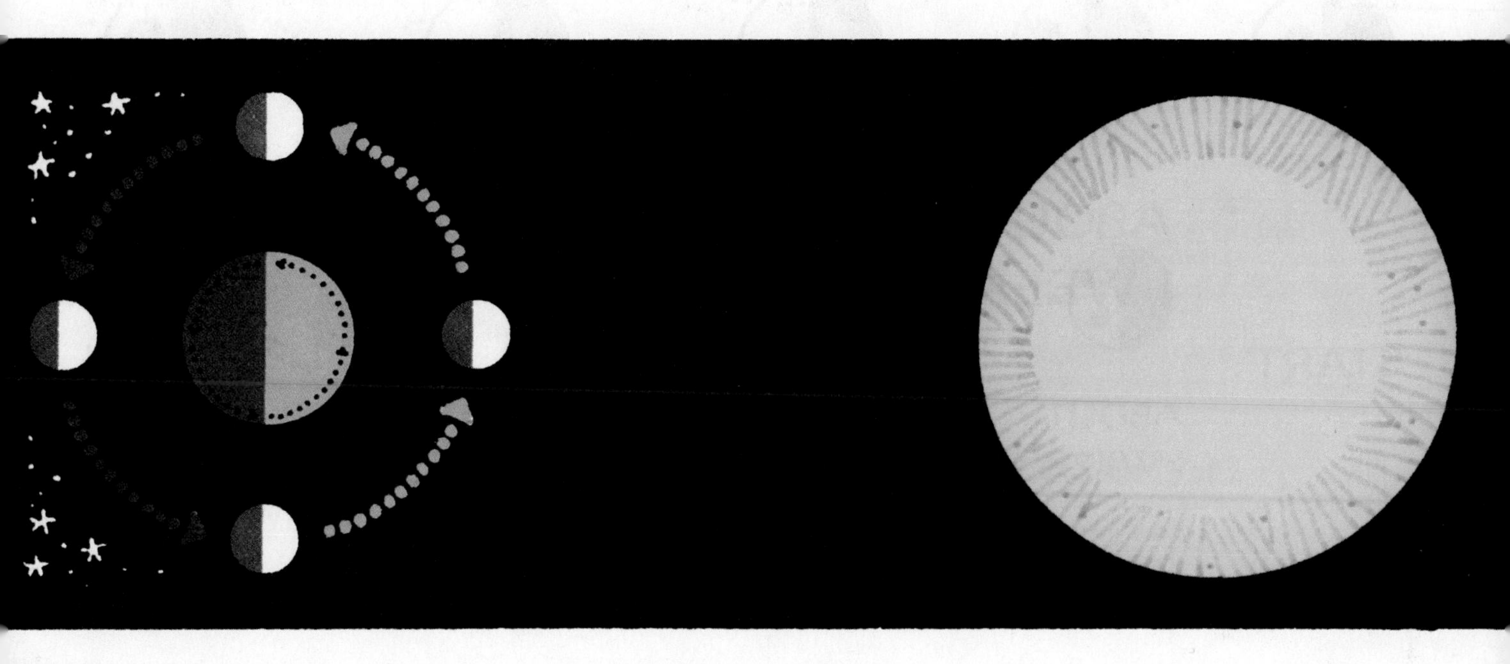

A day on Earth is 24 hours long.

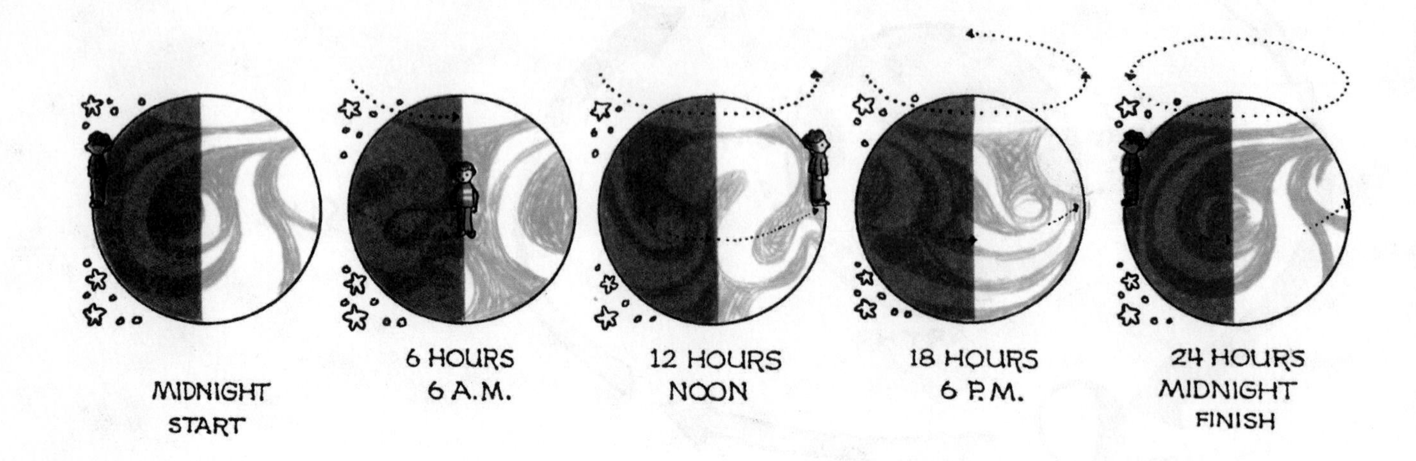

A day on the moon
is almost a month long.

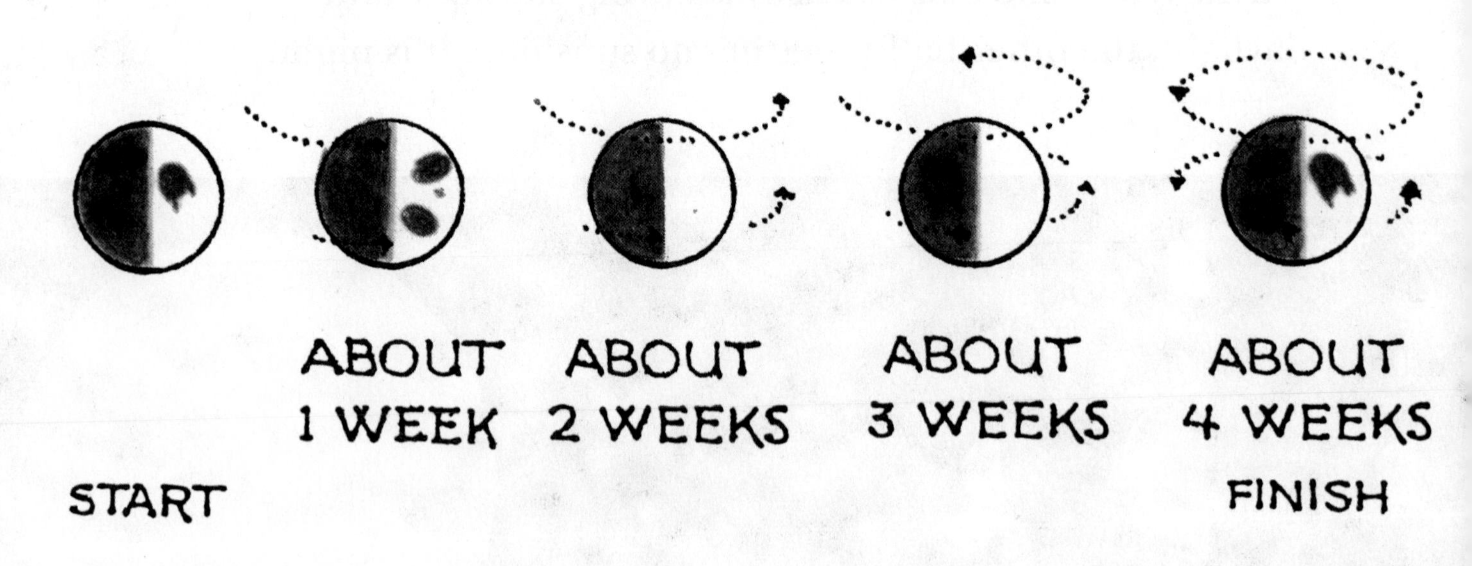

It takes the moon about
four weeks to go around Earth.

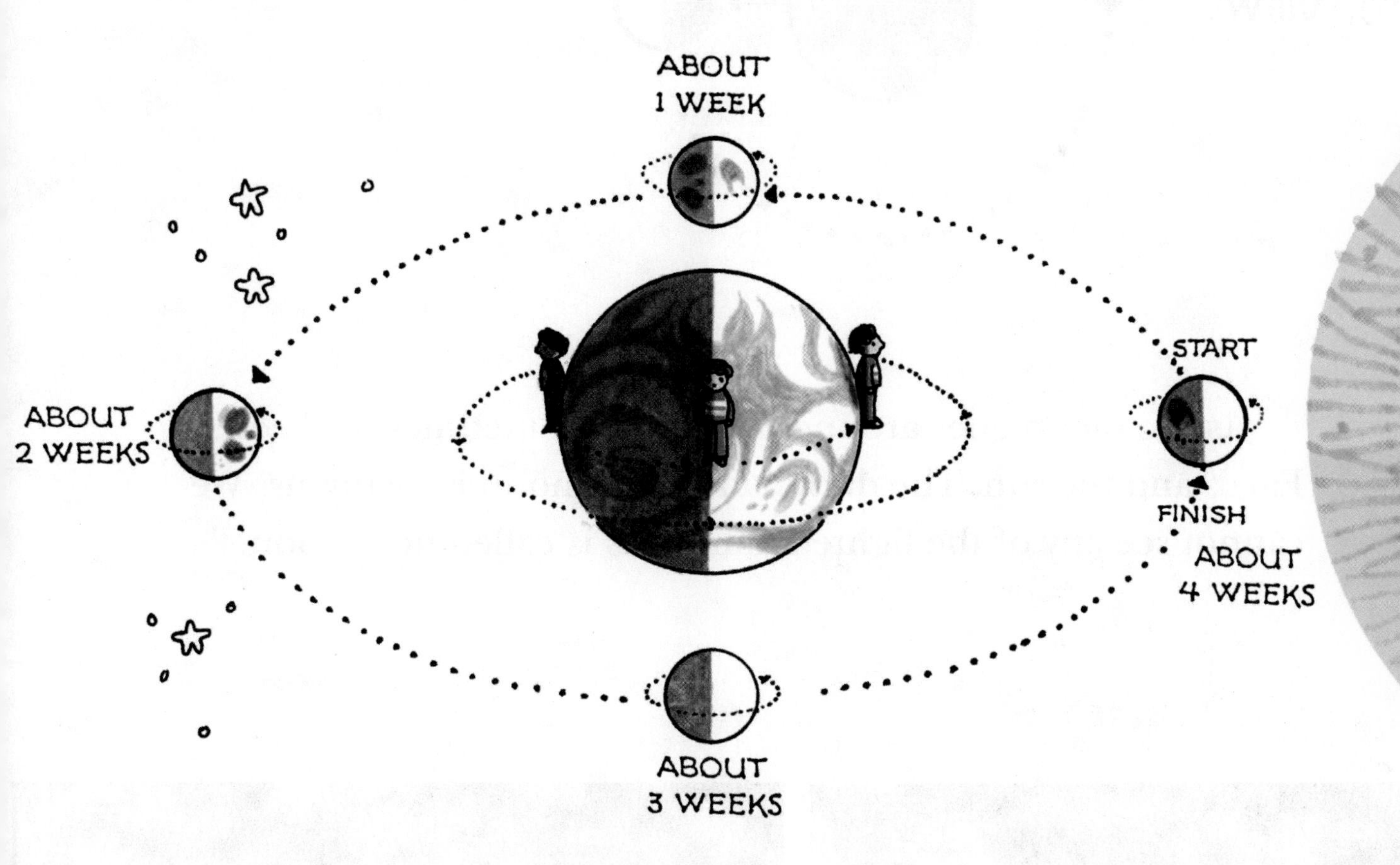

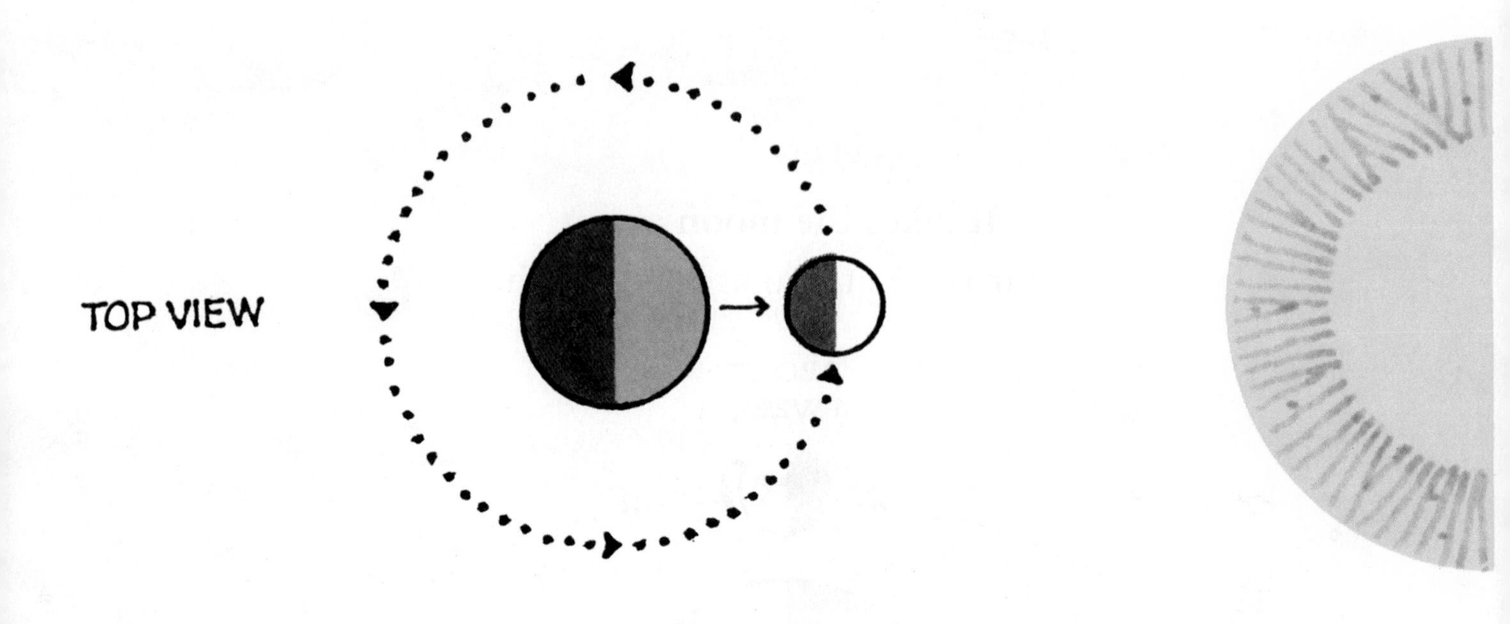

As the moon goes around Earth, it is sometimes between Earth and the sun. The dark half of the moon is facing us. We cannot see any of the lighted half. This is called new moon.

NIGHT
DAY
DARK SIDE OF MOON FACING US
SO WE CANNOT SEE IT.

NIGHT
DAY
NEW MOON NOT IN NIGHT SKY
SO WE CANNOT SEE IT.

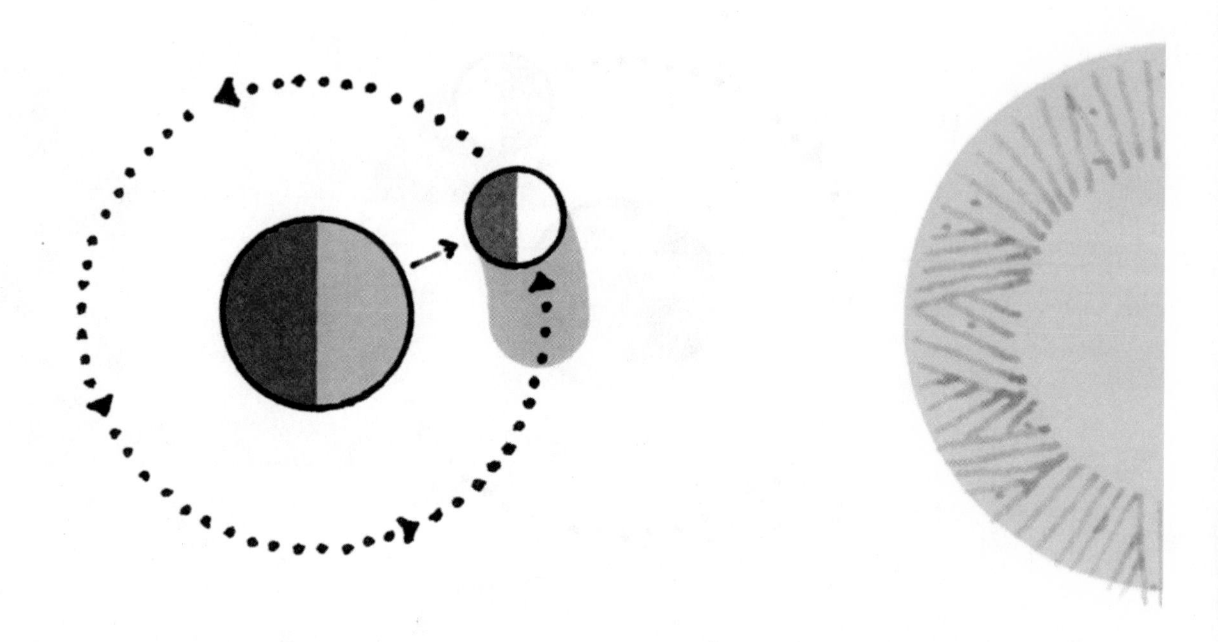

A night or two later the moon has moved a little bit along its path around Earth. We can then see a small part of the lighted half. It is called a crescent moon. We see it just after sunset. It is in the west, where we see the sun go down. You may be able to see it before the sky is dark. Sometimes you can see it in daytime.

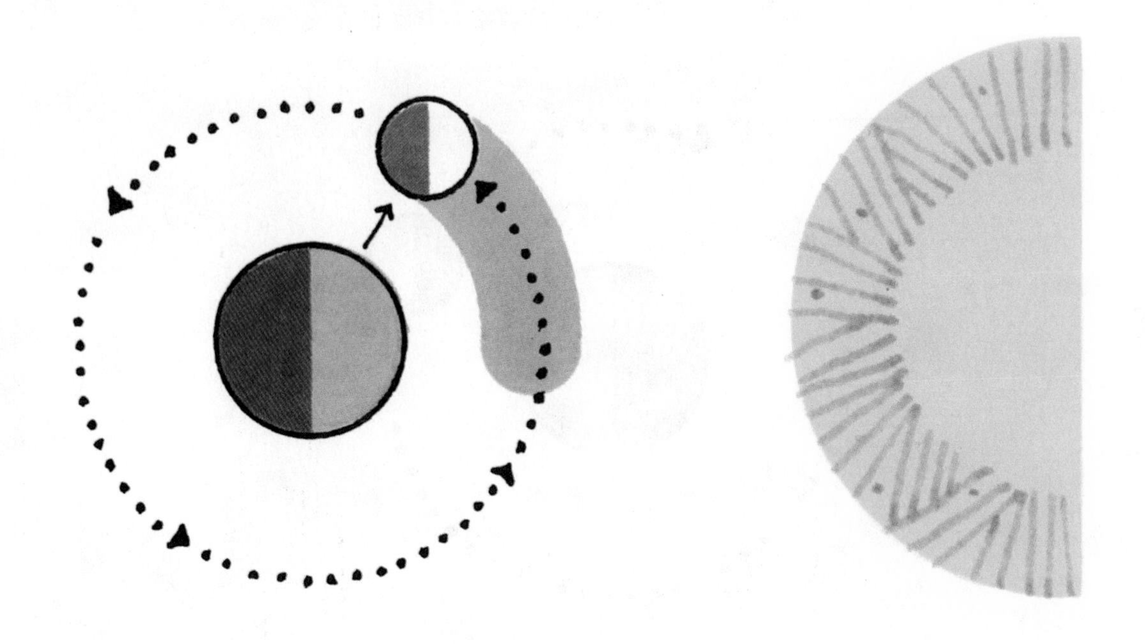

Each night the moon seems to grow. The moon is waxing. We can see a bit more of the lighted half.

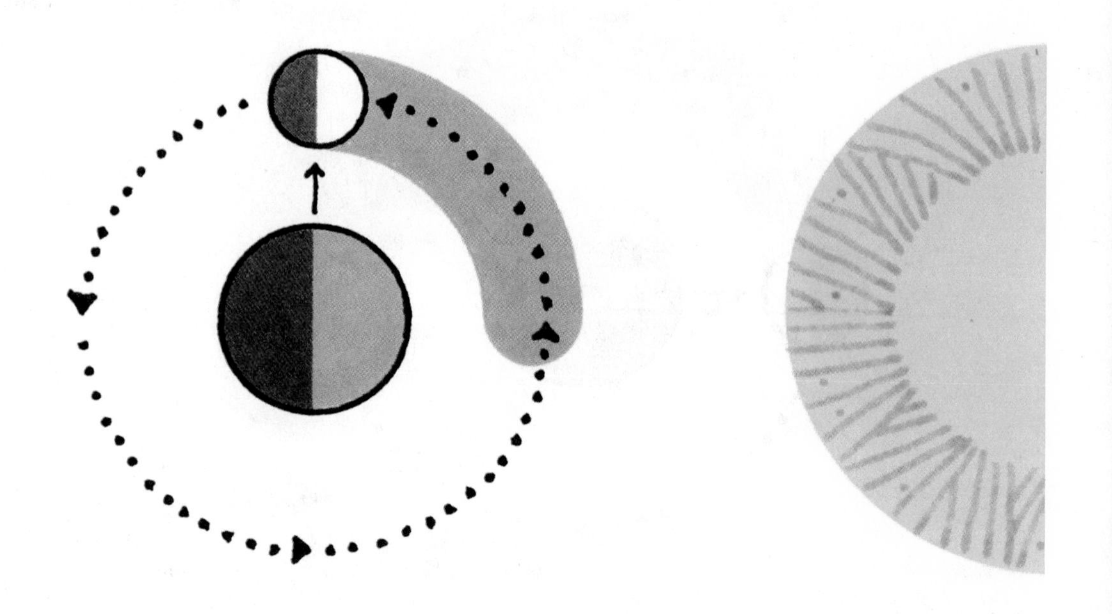

About a week after the moon is new, it has become a first-quarter moon. It looks like this. Sometimes you can see it in the afternoon before the sky is dark.

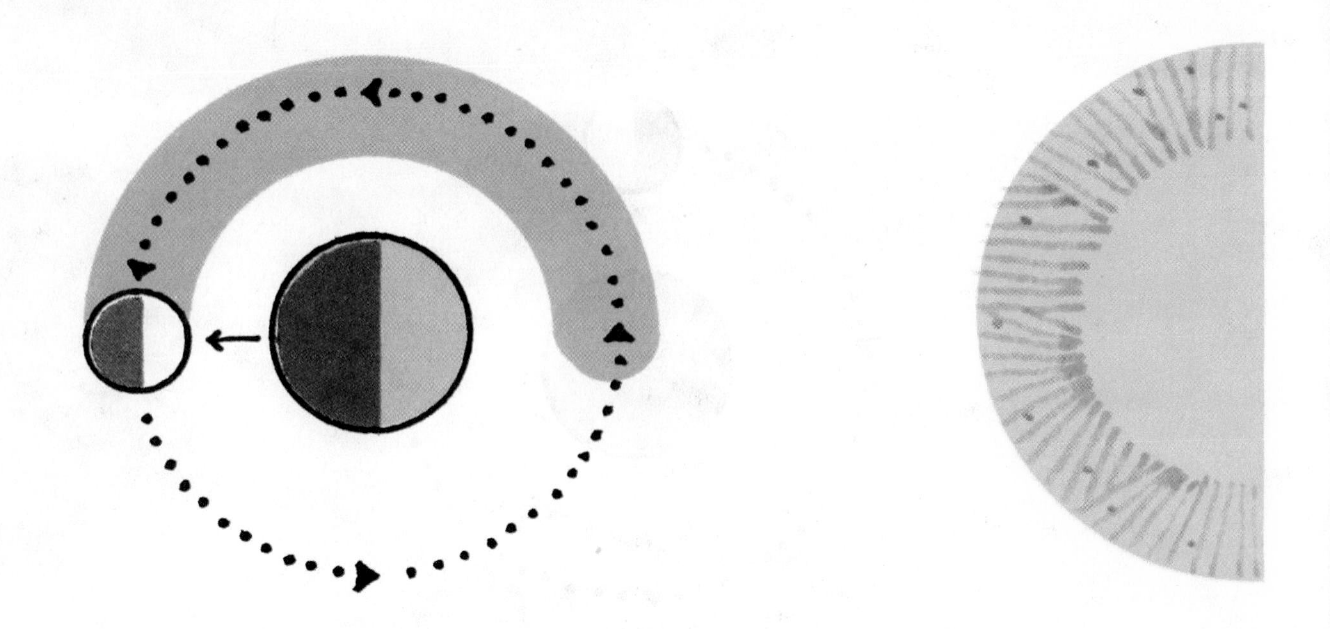

After another week the moon is on one side of Earth and the sun is on the other side. We can see all the lighted half of the moon. It is a full moon. We see it in the east as the sun sets in the west. We can't see it in the daytime.

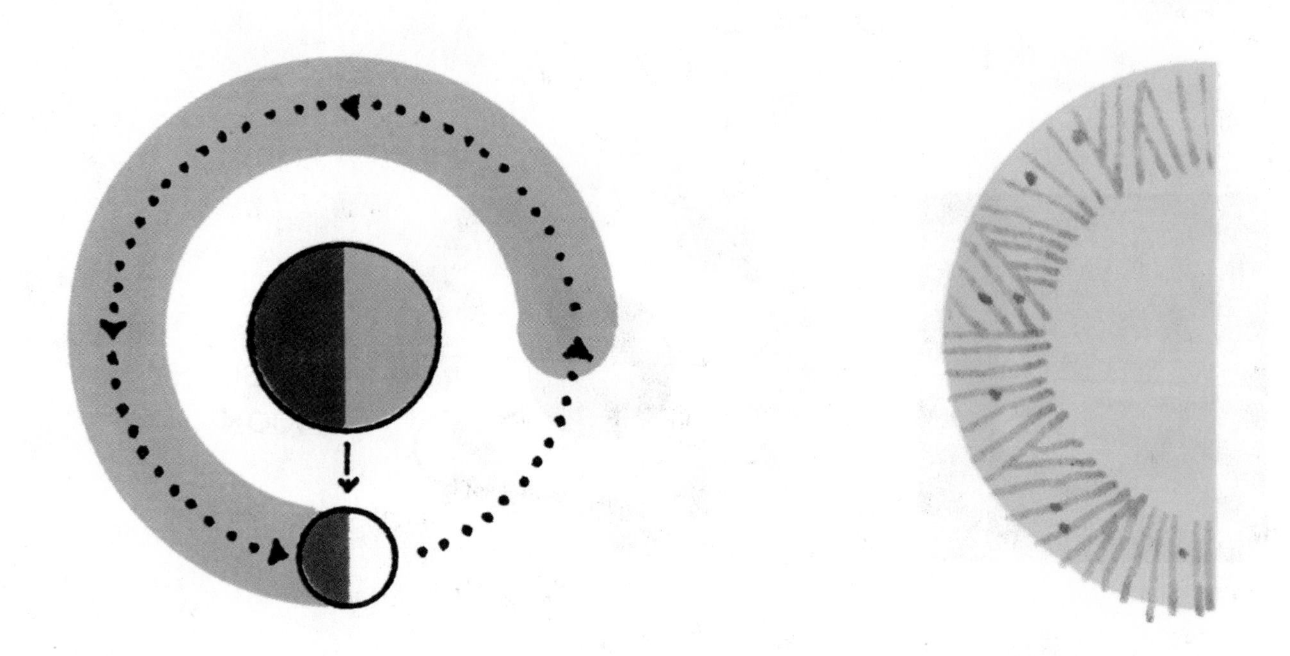

Each night after it is full, we see less and less of the moon. The moon is waning. In about a week it is a quarter moon. This is third quarter. It can be seen after midnight.

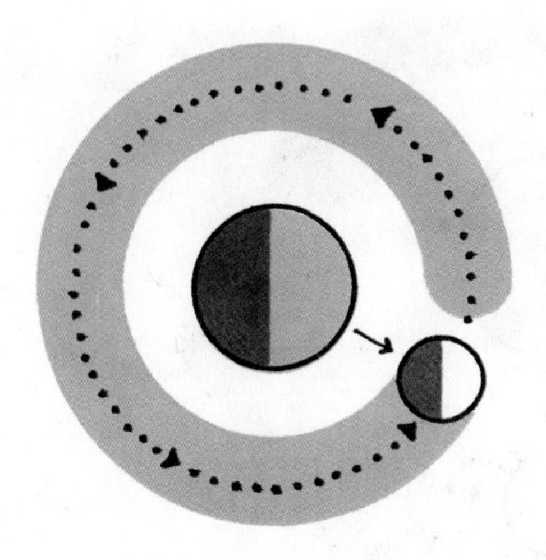

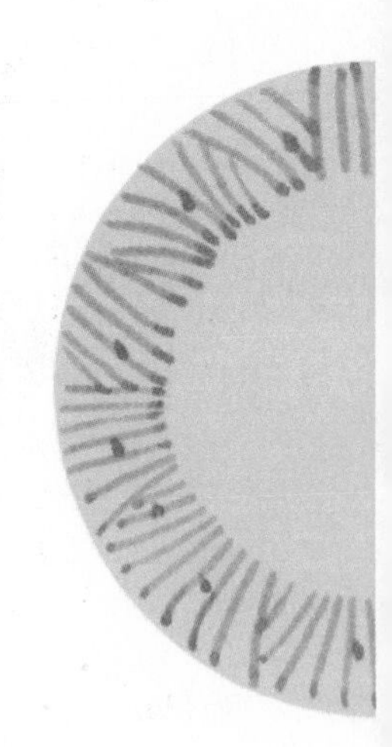

After that, the moon once more becomes a crescent. Each night the crescent gets a bit thinner. We would see it later and later at night—long after we're usually asleep. A few days later we cannot see the moon at all. It is once again a new moon. About four weeks after the moon is new, we have another new moon.

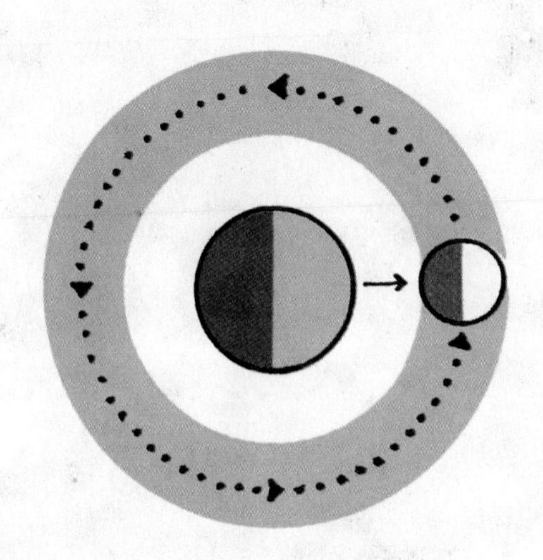

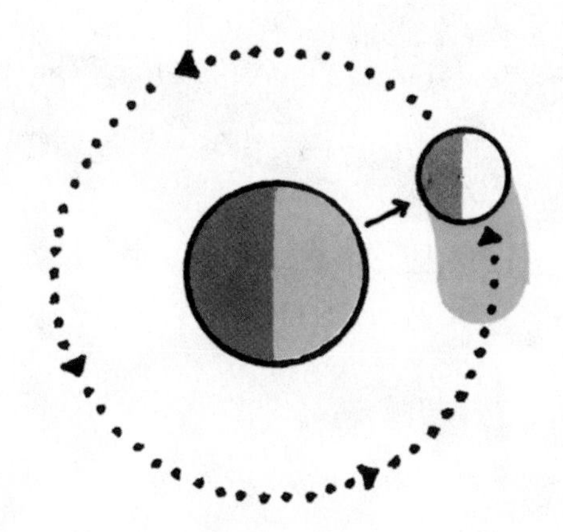

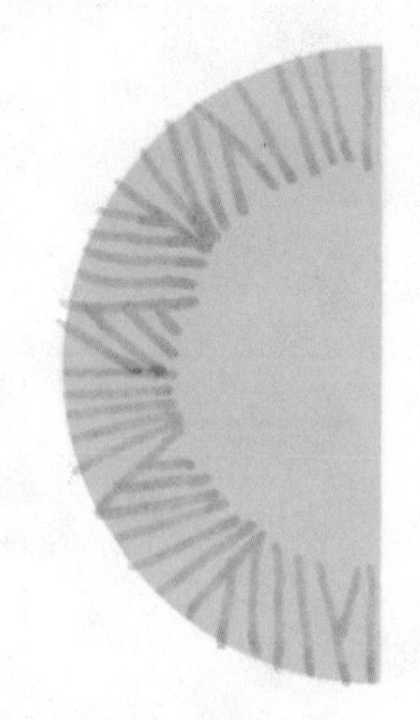

Two or three nights later, the moon has become a thin crescent. Night after night the same changes occur. Keep watch on the skies and you will see the changes—new moon, crescent, first quarter, full moon, third quarter, crescent and back to new moon. All together, the changes are called the phases of the moon.

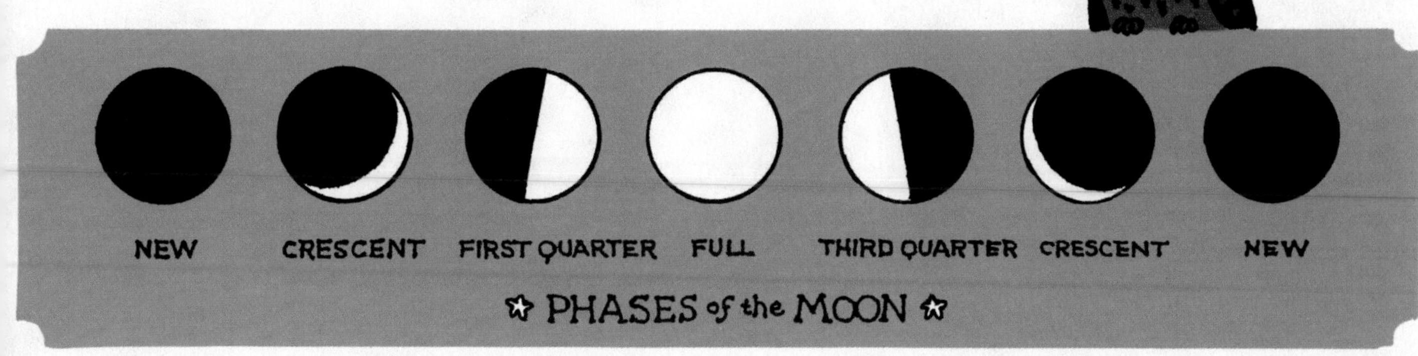

THIS IS THE SIDE
OF THE MOON
YOU CAN SEE
FROM THE EARTH.

Until spaceships went around the moon, we had never seen the other half of it.

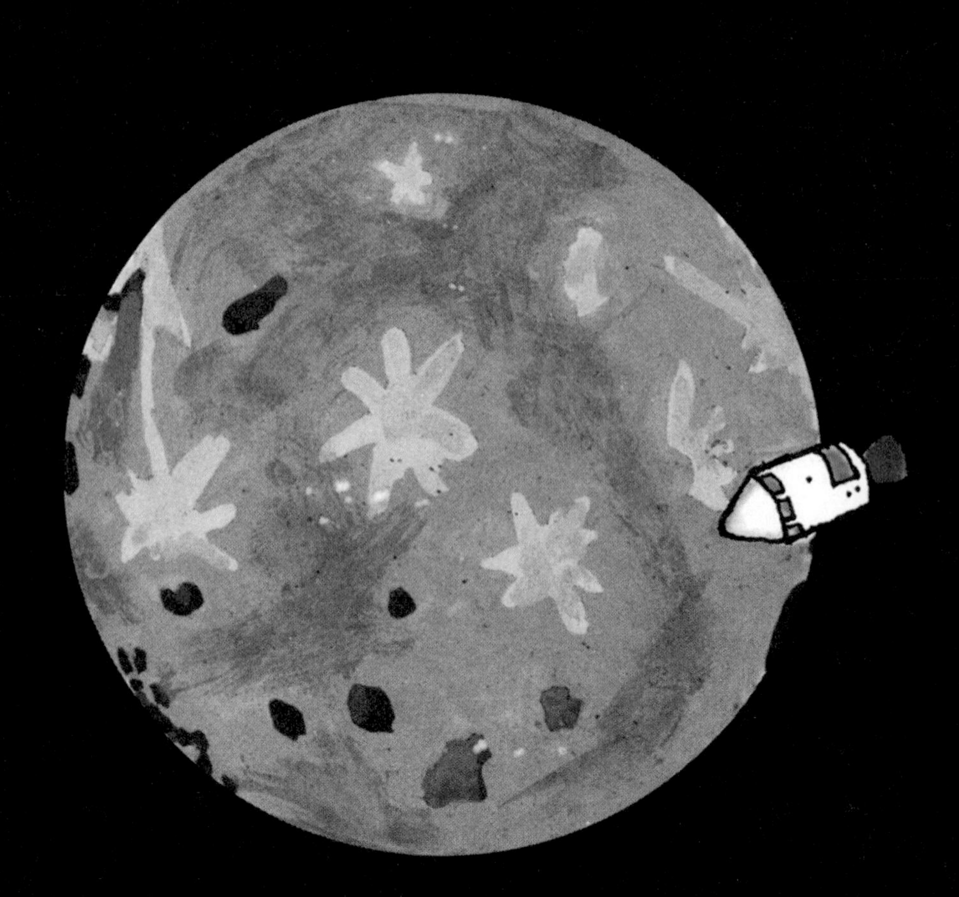

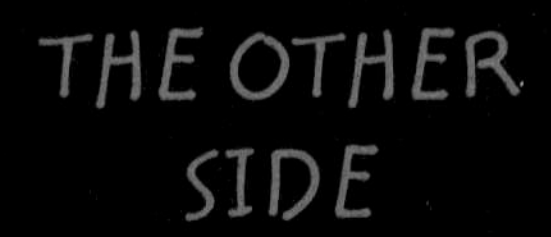

Sometimes we see a lot of the part of the moon that is turned toward us, and sometimes only a little of it. The moon grows bigger, and then gets smaller. The moon seems to change. It goes through phases because it goes around Earth.

Which phase of the moon can you see tonight?

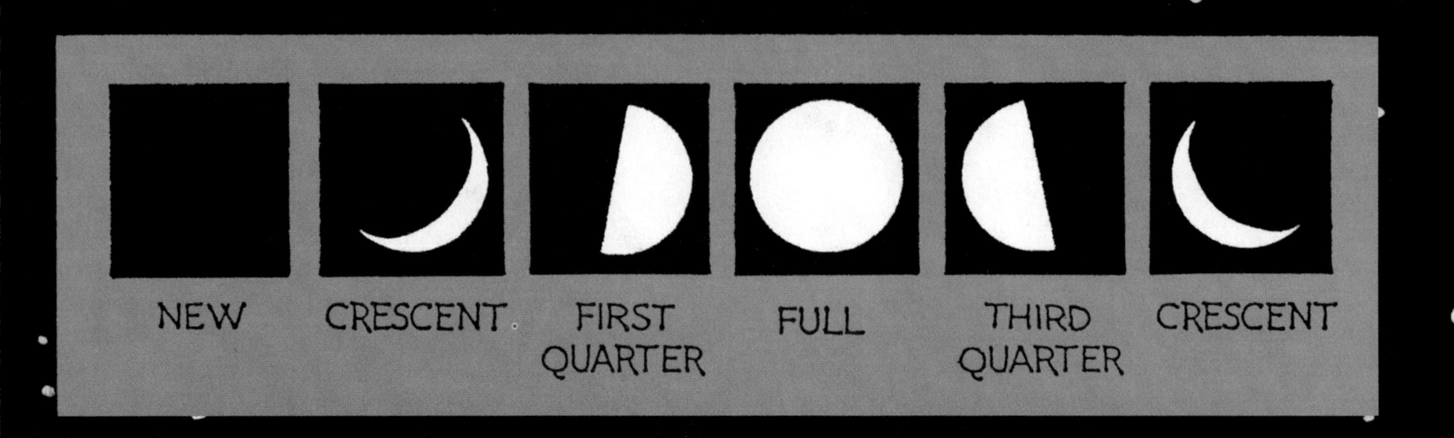

Brother

by Mary Ann Hoberman

I had a little brother
And I brought him to my mother
And I said I want another
Little brother for a change.

But she said don't be a bother
So I took him to my father
And I said this little bother
Of a brother's very strange.

But he said one little brother
Is exactly like another
And every little brother
Misbehaves a bit he said.

So I took the little brother
From my mother and my father
And I put the little bother
Of a brother back to bed.

Magnifying Glass

by Valerie Worth

Small grains
In a stone
Grow edges
That twinkle;

The smooth
Moth's wing
Sprouts feathers
Like shingles;

My thumb
Is wrapped
In rich
Satin wrinkles.

Rhyme

by Elizabeth Coatsworth

I like to see a thunder storm,
A dunder storm,
A blunder storm,
I like to see it, black and slow,
Come stumbling down the hills.

I like to hear a thunder storm,
A plunder storm,
A wonder storm,
Roar loudly at our little house
And shake the window sills!

Roots

by Douglas Florian

The roots of trees
Don't just grow **d**
o
w
n.

They **b r a n c h** out
Sideways, underground,
To help the tree to get a grip,
To anchor it so it won't slip.
As root hairs drink
The rain that **p**
o
u
r
s
They sip it up like tiny straws.
While by the growing roots in holes
Live badgers, rabbits, moles, and voles.
They tunnel under roots of trees
And *root* there for their families.

Under the Microscope

by Lee Bennett Hopkins

Unseen with
an unaided eye
amoebas
glide
on a small
glass slide.

Magnified
one thousand times
protozoans
split in two—

it's miraculous
what
a microscope
can do.

Summer Full Moon

by James Kirkup

The cloud tonight
is like a white
  Persian cat—

It lies among the stars
with eyes almost shut,
lapping the milk from
the moon's brimming dish.

The Moon is a White Cat

– from Hungary

The moon is a white cat
that hunts
the gray mice of night.

The Athabascans

Old Ways and New Ways

BY RON FRIDELL

What if you and a few dozen others were the only people for miles and miles? What if there were no cities or towns? What if everything around you was wild and winters were long and cold? How would you survive?

You would have to live like a pioneer. Long ago, pioneers migrated to a cold and wild land we now call Northern Alaska. They had to learn new skills and create a new way of life. And they did. These ancient Alaskan Natives were known as Athabascans (Ath·a·bas·cans).

Thousands of Athabascans live in Alaska today. Most live in cities and towns and drive cars and snowmachines. But not so long ago, many Athabascans chose to live in small villages along rivers. They wanted to live in the old ways, not the new ways. They wanted to learn and practice the skills passed down to them from their ancient Alaskan ancestors.

Finding Food

What was life like for the people in these villages? How did they adapt to this harsh and wild environment? Nothing came easy. They had to make the best use of everything they could get their hands on. Just like their ancestors.

First, they had to feed themselves. Fish was their major source of food. Most Athabascan villages were located along rivers full of salmon. To catch them, villagers would use nets, spears, and poles with hooks. Or they would set up fences to guide the fish into basket traps.

Ptarmigan

Arctic hare

Caribou

They even built wide, spinning fishwheels to scoop salmon from the river. They cut the fish into strips and used salt to preserve the meat. They also got meat by hunting and trapping wolves, beaver, muskrat, caribou, reindeer, moose, rabbits, and birds.

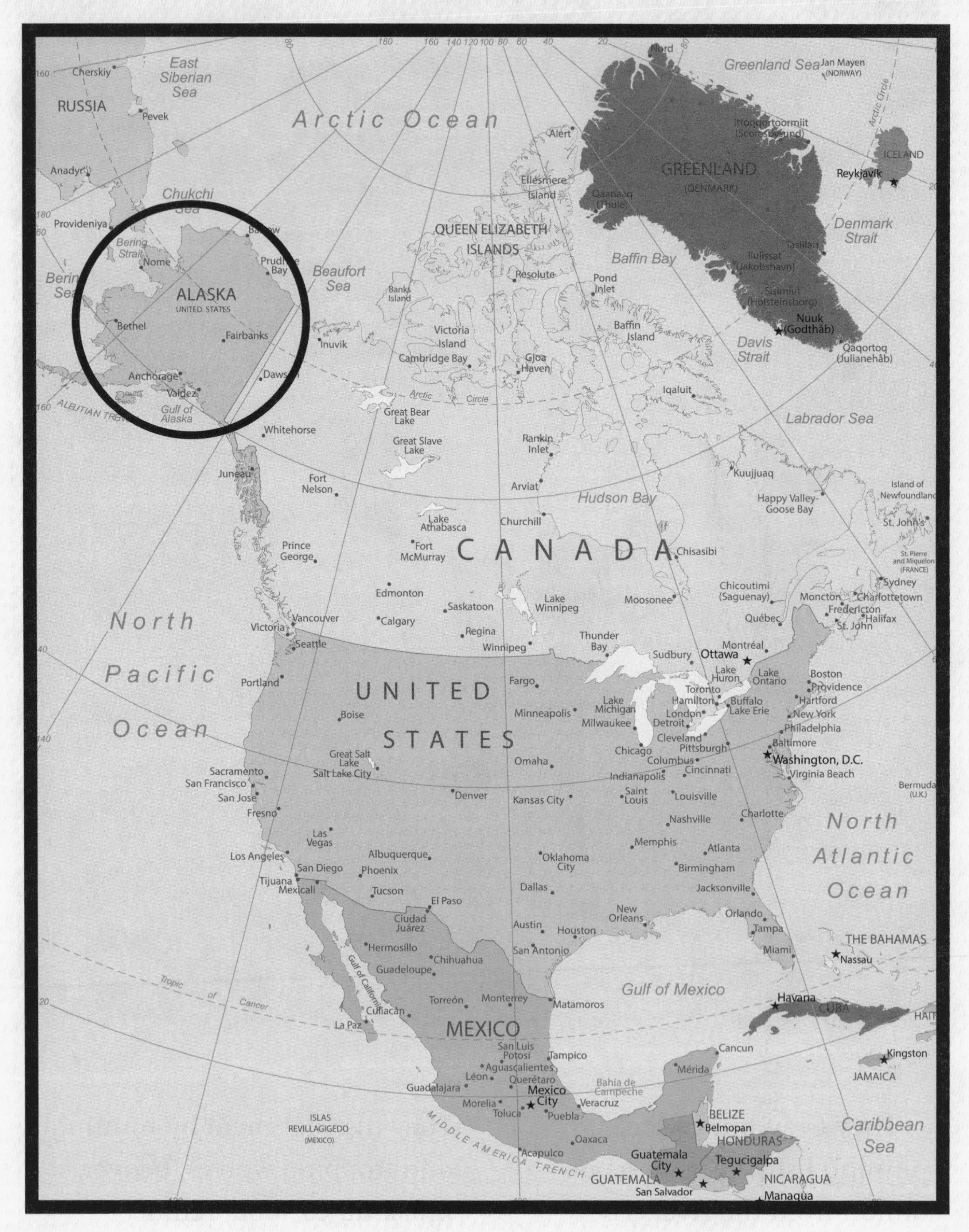

Alaska is the northernmost state of the United States.

Camping

The Athabascans who lived in villages had to be ready for the change of seasons. With each new season, many villagers would travel to a new hunting or fishing place and set up a camp there.

Athabascans dried fish for future use.

In summer they traveled along the river to where the salmon were most plentiful. In the fall they camped where they knew there were moose and caribou. In the spring they went to where lots of sweet wild berries grew. Camp life was good fun, but there was lots of work.

Even kids helped out. Older kids took care of babies while the adults were hard at work. One Athabascan woman shares her memories of fish camp along the Koyukuk River:

"We worked hard all summer on fishing. We set a fish net and checked it once or twice a day. My parents, aunts, uncles and older kids cut fish. The younger kids would also learn how to cut fish too. Younger kids helped by hanging fish, carrying water, and gathering wood. Cooking was also a big part of being in camp. We all had to chip in to make sure everyone was fed."

She says that the summers she spent in fish camp were some of the best times in her life. Everyone in her community knew everyone else, and they all cared for one another.

Staying Warm

The villagers used animals for more than just food. Animal hides and furs kept them warm in those cold Alaskan winters. They made soft winter boots called mukluks from moosehide and reindeer skin. They made winter gloves from moosehide and beaver fur. They turned caribou hide into warm pants, leggings, and shirts. They turned fur from wolves, muskrat, and wolverines into warm winter coats and parkas. Layers of fish skin made boots and parkas waterproof. Villagers also turned antlers and bones into knives and sewing needles. Just like their ancestors.

The ancestors believed that powerful spirits protected animals. These spirits expected the people to treat animals with respect. If not, the spirits would make the animals go away. So the ancestors set up strict rules for hunting, killing, and eating animals. And many villagers still honored their ancestors' rules.

Mukluks

Hard Winters

Winters were long and cold. In the other seasons villagers could live in cabins. But winter meant staying in a house that kept the heat in and the cold wind out. These winter houses were half underground. That way no heat from the stove or fireplace could escape through windows or walls.

The roof was covered by a layer of logs, a layer of moss, and a layer of sod. From outside, the house looked like a great big mound of snow with smoke coming up from the chimney.

Animals were scarce in winter. Villagers would have to live on food stored up from the rest of the year. For water, they would have to melt snow or chunks of ice from the frozen river.

Getting Around

People used dogsleds to get around in winter, or they walked from place to place on snowshoes pulling toboggans. The rest of the year they went on foot or traveled by water in canoes made from birch trees.

But what about long distance travel? These villages did not have roads leading to cities and towns. The outside world was far away. For a long time the only way to reach the villages was by river.

That changed in the 1920s when bush planes came flying in. These little planes had landing gear for every kind of place. Some had skis to take off and land in snow. Some had pontoons for rivers or lakes. Others had wheels for flat, grassy landing fields.

The planes brought mail. They brought supplies such as oil for lamps, batteries for radios, pots and pans, and medicines. They brought people, such as visitors who came to see relatives and friends, and doctors to treat the sick. They even brought school teachers.

One-Room Schoolhouses

Not all villages had schools back then. Sometimes the villagers had to join together and build a school themselves. Each school had to have at least six students. Some small villages did not even have that many. So children from two or three villages would all go to the same school. One man remembers walking two miles each way to his school when he was little. This could get scary in the spring and fall, he said. He would have to watch out for all the big hungry bears looking for berries in the woods.

All the grades, first through eighth, were taught in one room all at once. One student remembers being the only seventh grade student on the school honor role. But then, he was also the only seventh grader in school that year!

Back then, about 60 years ago, schools used lanterns for light, a wood or oil stove for heat, and a barrel with a dipper for water. The bathroom was in a little building outside. One teacher remembers seeing fierce-looking wolves prowling around the school. When it got dark, she said, "We always traveled in pairs clutching flashlights. Green, fiery wolf orbs glared back at us from the surrounding darkness."

For these Athabascans, living out in the wilds was an adventure. It was all an education. They learned the old ways and practiced them. But that didn't stop them from learning the new ways of a new world in school, even if the school had only a single room.

THE FROG PRINCESS

A TLINGIT LEGEND FROM ALASKA

retold by Eric A. Kimmel
illustrated by Rosanne Litzinger

Many Years Ago, a Tlingit village stood on the shores of a beautiful lake. The village headman was a person of wealth and power. His daughter was one of the most beautiful girls in the Tlingit nation. Many young men came to the village, hoping to make her their bride. They brought rich presents for the girl and her father. However, neither the gifts nor any of the young men were ever good enough for her.

"Marry you? Why I would sooner marry a frog from our lake!" she told one suitor whose eyes bulged slightly. Everyone in the village laughed. The poor young man left in disgrace and never returned.

That night the headman's daughter woke from a sound sleep. She heard someone knocking. Dressing quickly, she tiptoed to the door and opened it.

A young man stood on the threshold. A green blanket covered his shoulders. His clothes and fine headdress were also green. The headman's daughter thought he was extremely handsome, though his eyes bulged slightly and his fingers seemed unusually long.

The young man spoke:

"Did you mean what you said this morning, that you would rather marry a frog from the lake than any of the suitors who have come to your village?"

"Yes," the girl replied.

The young man held out his hand. "Then come with me."

The girl walked with him to the edge of the lake. The young man took hold of the water. He lifted it up as if it were the corner of a blanket. The girl saw steps leading to the lake bottom.

"You go first. I will follow," the young man said.

Together they walked down and down until they reached the bottom of the lake. The Frog People came to greet them. They were all very handsome, though their eyes bulged slightly and their fingers seemed unusually long.

"Welcome, Daughter," the frog chief said. "This is your new home and we are your new family. We are the Frog People."

The Frog People led her to a large cedar house. Here they held a wedding feast in her honor. The girl enjoyed the feasting and dancing so much that she forgot about time. Weeks passed. Yet it seemed to the girl that she had been gone only a few hours.

The headman and his wife awoke to find their daughter gone. They searched through the village. They combed the forests and the seashore. They found not a clue. It was as if their daughter had disappeared from the earth. The headman held a funeral feast. The whole village mourned his daughter as if she were dead.

One morning a traveler came to the village. He asked to speak to the headman. He told an unusual story.

"Last night I camped on the far side of the lake. At dusk I heard a young woman's voice singing. I followed the sound. It led me to a marsh. There I saw a beautiful girl sitting on a log, surrounded by frogs. They were all singing and dancing together. This seemed strange to me. Can you explain it?"

The headman asked the traveler to describe the young woman. When he did so, the headman recognized her at once. It was his daughter.

"Take me to the place where you saw these things," he told the traveler. Together they set out for the far side of the lake.

The headman walked along the lake's shore. He stood on the edge of the marsh.

"Chief of the Frog People!" he called out. "Come out of the water. I must speak with you."

The waters of the lake began to stir. A giant frog hopped out onto the beach. "What do you want?" he croaked.

"I want my daughter," the village headman said. "Give her back if she is with you. You have no right to keep her without her parents' consent."

"She is happy with us," the frog chief replied. "She has a husband and many, many children. If you let her stay with us, we will give you great gifts in exchange."

"Keep your gifts. I want my daughter," the headman repeated. "If you do not give her up, there will be war between your people and mine. We will dig ditches to drain this lake. When the water is gone, your people will have to leave. I will find my daughter and take her."

The frog chief blinked his eyes. "The Frog People do not want war. I will bring your daughter back. Return to this spot tomorrow. Your daughter will be here."

The headman went back to the lake the next day. As the frog chief had promised, his daughter stood waiting for him on the beach. She appeared to be in good health, though her eyes bulged slightly and her fingers had grown unusually long. She was dressed in beautiful clothes. A large pile of gifts lay at her feet.

When the headman brought his daughter home, he discovered that she could not speak. The only sounds she made were the croaks of a frog. Her parents prepared a salmon feast in her honor. She did not touch a morsel. She sat with her eyes lowered, looking very sad.

The girl's strange behavior worried her parents. They sent for the shaman. He prepared a healing mixture of roots and herbs to drive out the bad spirits inside her. The girl drank the potion. Suddenly she vomited out a great ball of mud. The shaman broke the ball apart. It was filled with the remains of worms and insects.

"This is the food she ate when she lived with the Frog People," the shaman explained. "Now that she has brought it up, she will be human again."

The shaman's words proved true. The girl looked around, as if she had awakened from a dream. She spoke in human language once more. However, she still seemed sad.

"I was happy at the bottom of the lake," she told her parents. "The Frog People were kind to me. I miss my husband and children. Why did you take me away from them?"

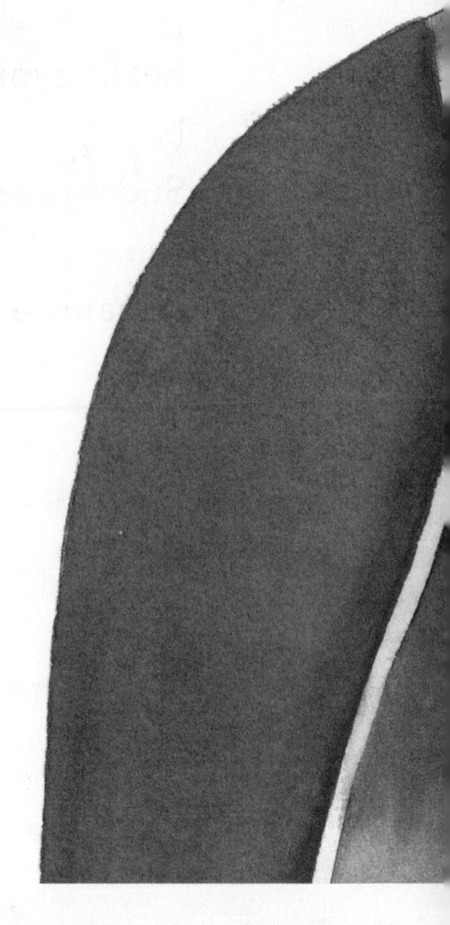

Her parents tried to explain. "We love you too. You are our daughter, and we missed you. It is unnatural for a human girl to live among frogs. They must marry their own kind, and so must you. We will find another husband for you. You will have more children, human children. Forget those frogs. You are back among human beings now, where you belong."

But the girl would not be comforted. Every evening she walked down to the lake. She sat beside its waters, not saying a word.

One day she did not return. The people of her village searched all around the lake. They paddled their canoes back and forth across its waters, but not a trace of her could they find.

The headman went to the lake's shore. Once again he called to the chief of the Frog People. But no one came. The frog chief did not answer his summons. Nor, from that time on, were frogs ever seen in that lake.

But it is also told that once, long after these events, a traveler passing through the mountains camped beside another, hidden lake. That night, as he prepared his dinner, a frog hopped into the light of the campfire. She spoke to him.

"When you come to a certain village, ask to speak to the headman. Tell him that his daughter is well, that she is happy here with her husband and children." Having said these words, the frog jumped back into the water. The traveler saw her no more.

That evening, as the traveler later told the headman, he heard a great number of frogs calling to one another back and forth across the lake. They croaked and peeped, as frogs do. But strange to tell, he added, when he shut his eyes and listened closely, he found he could understand what they were saying. For the frogs were all talking in Tlingit.

City Homes

by Nicola Barber

What is a city home?

A city is a place where thousands, sometimes millions, of people live and work. There are many buildings in a city, such as offices, stores, factories, and homes.

▼ *About six million people live in the city of Rio de Janeiro, Brazil, in South America.*

Cities can be very crowded places. Some people live in large houses. Many people live in tall buildings that contain a lot of homes. These are called "apartment buildings."

◀ *These houses are in San Francisco, California. There are office buildings in the distance.*

City life

The world's tallest building is in the city of Dubai in the United Arab Emirates. It is 2,717 feet (828 meters) high!

Townhouses and suburbs

In some cities, the streets are lined with houses that are all joined together in a long line. These are called "townhouses" or "terraced houses."

▼ *Rows of townhouses line the edge of the River Seine in Paris, France.*

Many people have their homes outside of the city center in areas called "suburbs." The suburbs are often located many miles from the city center. Despite their distance, they are still part of the city.

▲ *These houses are in the suburbs of Stockholm, the capital city of Sweden.*

Building a city home

Many city people live in apartment buildings. These tall towers are made from steel, concrete, and glass. Builders use the steel to make a strong frame for the building. They use the concrete and glass to make the walls and windows.

▼ *People have no gardens in these apartments in Wuhan, China. Their balconies are the only outside spaces.*

In other places, city homes are built using materials found nearby, such as mud or stone. People mix the mud with straw to make the building stronger.

▲ *Many of the mud houses in Kano, Nigeria, have decorations on their roofs.*

The weather

In very hot places, people try to keep their city homes cool. In some cities, buildings have wind catchers on top. These wind catchers are like wide chimneys facing toward the wind. They trap the wind, and the air goes into the rooms below.

▼ *The city of Yazd, Iran, lies in the middle of a hot desert. Wind catchers help cool houses there.*

It can get very cold during the winter in some cities. The city of Moscow, Russia, has snow on its streets in winter. Hot water is pumped through pipes to keep homes warm. People turn on electric radiators when the temperature drops very low.

City life

In 2006, the temperature went as low as -36° Fahrenheit (-38° Celsius) in Moscow.

▲ *Winter in Moscow is so cold that canals and rivers freeze over.*

School and play

City schools can be very big, with hundreds of students. Some children may have come to the city from other countries. Students at a school may know many different languages.

▼ *These girls are using computers at a school in New York City.*

There are many different things to do in a city. Children can visit parks and city zoos. There are theaters and cinemas for going to see plays and films. There are libraries for reading books. There are swimming pools and places for playing sports.

▲ *Actors perform a play outdoors in a park in Melbourne, Australia.*

Getting around

There are many different ways to travel around a city. Some cities have trains called "subways" that go through tunnels underground. Other cities have streetcars that run on rails in the streets.

▼ *People are getting on and off of a subway train in Hamburg, Germany.*

Many people drive cars in cities. City streets are often full of cars. Sometimes, cars stuck in traffic move so slowly that it takes a long time to go even a short distance.

▲ *Cars and other vehicles are stuck in a long traffic jam on this street in Kolkata, India.*

Arctic Sun

by Eileen Spinelli

In early June the Arctic sun
illuminates the day.
It spangles melting ice
and lingering snow.
It sparkles on the wings
of glaucous gull
who's come to nest
and watch her babies grow.

In early June the Arctic sun
holds to the sky
and plays the part of moon
throughout the night.
It shimmers on the dreams
of Arctic hare
and splashes sleepy weasel
with its light.

Ptarmigan

by Eileen Spinelli

Most other birds
Who soar with summery grace
Depart when Arctic winter
Shows its face.
Not the ptarmigan.

She stays,
With feathery snowshoes
On her feet
And sometimes only
Buds from twigs to eat.
Hardy ptarmigan.

Then finding space
Behind a heap of rocks,
She sleeps and hides
From hungry Arctic fox.
O ever clever ptarmigan.

Caribou

by Eileen Spinelli

Across the tundra
Caribou coming.
Racing and chasing
Caribou coming.
Thrumming and drumming
Caribou coming.
Romping and stomping
Caribou coming.
Hammering, clamoring
Caribou coming.
Thundering, rumbling
Caribou coming.
In waves, cascades
Caribou coming
and coming
    and coming
        and coming
            and coming.

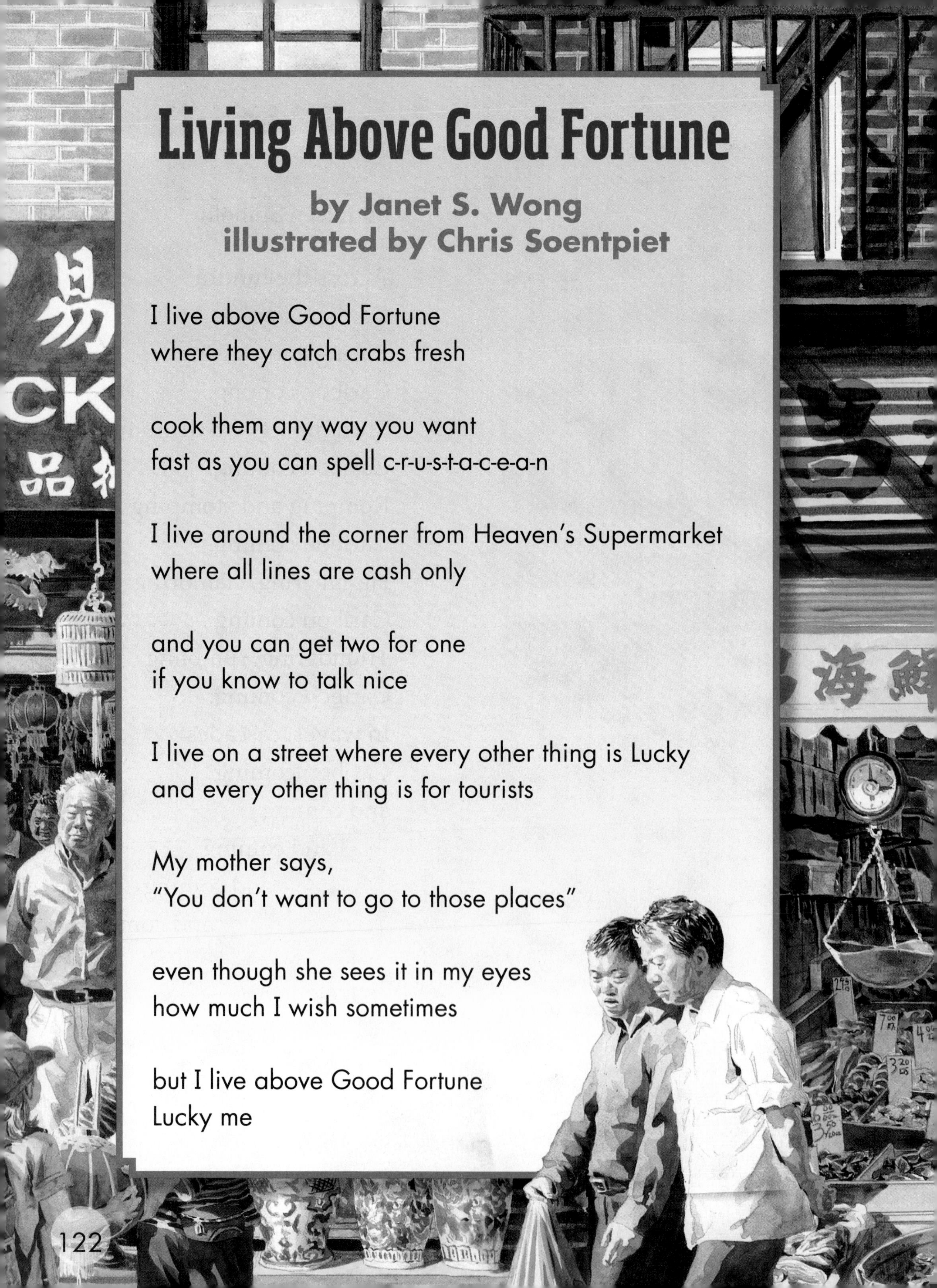

Living Above Good Fortune

by Janet S. Wong
illustrated by Chris Soentpiet

I live above Good Fortune
where they catch crabs fresh

cook them any way you want
fast as you can spell c-r-u-s-t-a-c-e-a-n

I live around the corner from Heaven's Supermarket
where all lines are cash only

and you can get two for one
if you know to talk nice

I live on a street where every other thing is Lucky
and every other thing is for tourists

My mother says,
"You don't want to go to those places"

even though she sees it in my eyes
how much I wish sometimes

but I live above Good Fortune
Lucky me

GOOD FO
EAFOOD MAR

場公司 GOOD FORTUNE SEAF

Walking Home from School

by Ann Whitford Paul

Grandpa Stokes calls out from his porch,
"Your backpack looks mighty full."
"Just like always," I say.

Mrs. Sanchez, working in her garden, says,
"Take a flower to your mother."
I pick my favorite daffodil.

Mrs. Carter climbs into her van.
"I forgot something for supper."
I laugh and think, Again!

Julie Kim is on the telephone.
She gives me the thumbs-up sign.
That means her boyfriend's calling.

Mr. Potner hammers at his workbench.
"How's it going, Lauren?"
He asks the same thing every day.

On my street as far as I can see
I know everyone.
Everyone knows me.

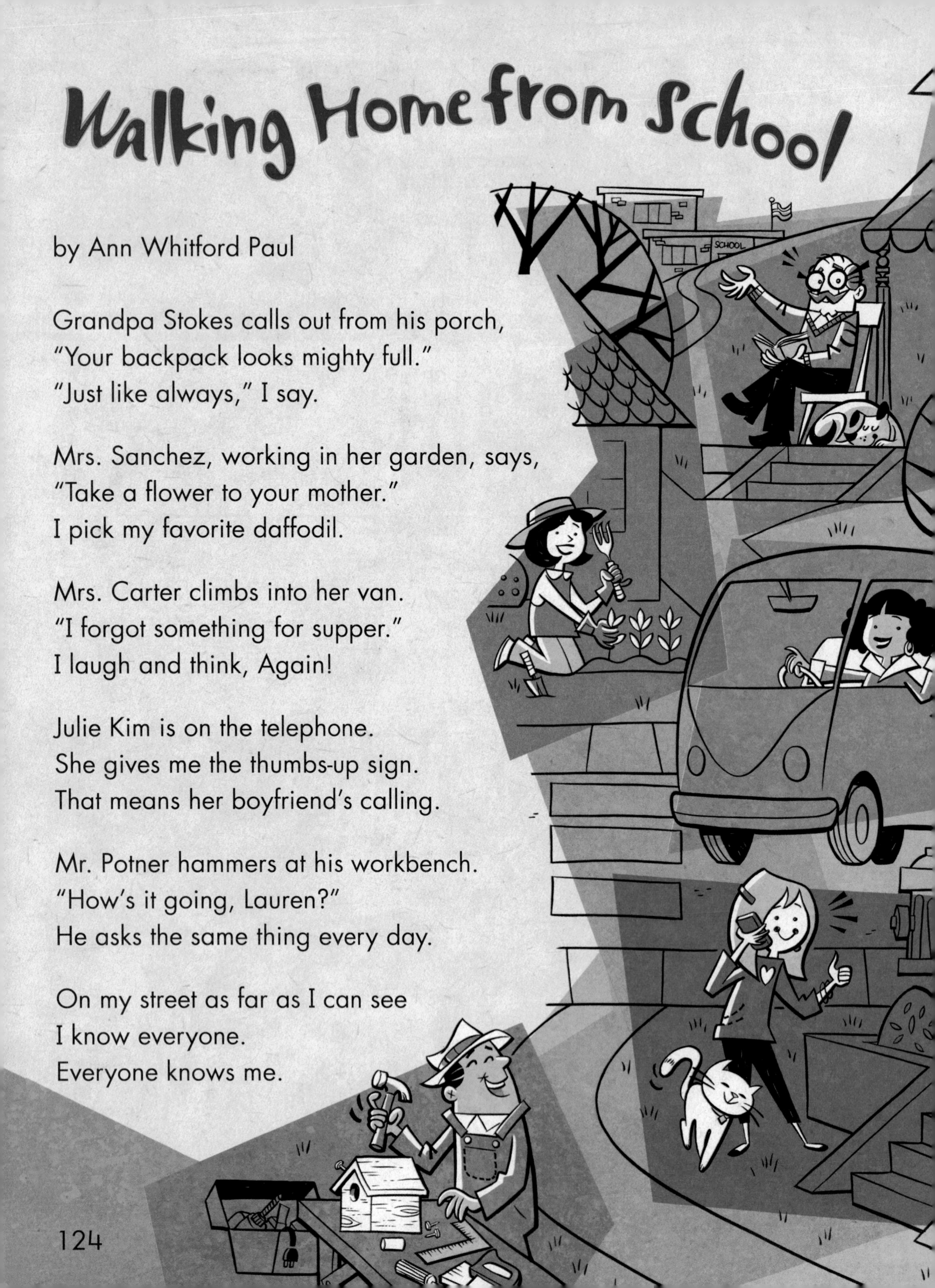

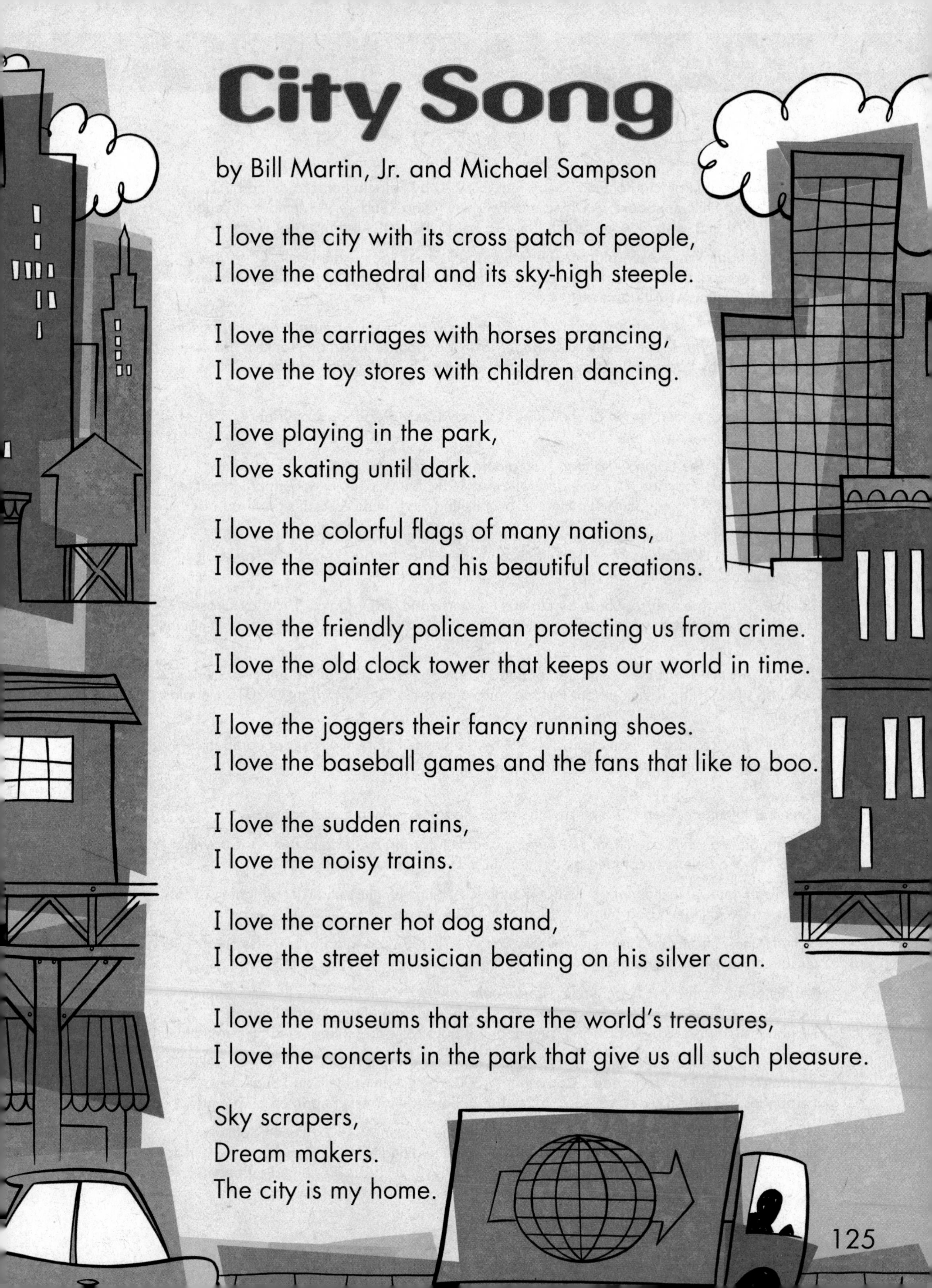

City Song

by Bill Martin, Jr. and Michael Sampson

I love the city with its cross patch of people,
I love the cathedral and its sky-high steeple.

I love the carriages with horses prancing,
I love the toy stores with children dancing.

I love playing in the park,
I love skating until dark.

I love the colorful flags of many nations,
I love the painter and his beautiful creations.

I love the friendly policeman protecting us from crime.
I love the old clock tower that keeps our world in time.

I love the joggers their fancy running shoes.
I love the baseball games and the fans that like to boo.

I love the sudden rains,
I love the noisy trains.

I love the corner hot dog stand,
I love the street musician beating on his silver can.

I love the museums that share the world's treasures,
I love the concerts in the park that give us all such pleasure.

Sky scrapers,
Dream makers.
The city is my home.

Text

Thunder Cake by Patricia Polacco. Copyright © 1990 by Patricia Polacco. Used by permission of Philomel Books, A Division of Penguin Young Readers, A Member of Penguin Group (USA) Inc., 345 Hudson Street, New York, NY 10014. All rights reserved.

"The Lemonade War," excerpt from *The Lemonade War* by Jacqueline Davis. Copyright © 2007 by Jacqueline Davis. Reprinted by arrangement with Houghton Mifflin Harcourt Publishing Company. All rights reserved.

"The Moon Seems to Change" by Franklyn Branley, illustrations by Barbara Emberly and Ed Emberley, from *The Moon Seems to Change.* Text Copyright © 1987 by Franklyn Branley, illustrations © by Barbara Emberly and Ed Emberly. Use by permission of HarperCollins Publishers.

"Brother," used by permission of The Gina Maccoby Literary Agency. Copyright © 1959 by Mary Ann Hoberman.

"Brother," from *The Llama Who Had No Pajama: 100 Favorite Poems* by Mary Ann Hoberman. Text copyright © 1959 and renewed 1987 by Mary Ann Hoberman. Reprinted by permission of Houghton Mifflin Harcourt Publishing Company. All rights reserved.

"magnifying glass," from *All the Small Poems and Fourteen More.* Copyright © 1987 by Valerie Worth. Illustrations © by Natalie Babbitt. Reprinted by permission of Henry Holt & Company, LLC. All rights reserved.

"Rhyme," from *The Sparrow Bush* by Elizabeth Coatsworth, copyright © 1966 by Grosset & Dunlap, Inc., renewed. Used by permission of Grosset & Dunlap, Inc., a division of Penguin Group (USA) LLC.

"Roots," reprinted with the permission of Beach Lane Books, an imprint of Simon & Schuster Children's Publishing Division from *Poetrees* by Douglas Florian. Copyright © 2010 Douglas Florian.

"Under the Microscope," copyright © 1999 by Lee Bennett Hopkins. First appeared in *Spectacular Science,* published by Simon & Schuster, Inc. Reprinted by permission of Curtis Brown, Ltd.

"Summer full moon," reprinted by permission of the James Kirkup Collection.

"The moon is a white cat," from *The Sun Is a Golden Earring* by Natalia Belting. Copyright © 1990 Natalia Belting. Reprinted by permission of Henry Holt & Company.

The Frog Princess. Text copyright © 2006 by Eric A. Kimmel. Illustrations copyright © 2006 by Rosanne Litzinger. Used by permission of Holiday House, Inc.

"City Homes," from City Homes by Nicola Barber, ©2008. Reprinted by permission of Crabtree Publishing Company.

"Arctic Sun," from *Polar Bear, Arctic Hare: Poems of the Frozen North* by Eileen Spinelli, illustrated by Eugenie Fernandes. Copyright © 2007 by Eileen Spinelli and Eugenie Fernandes. Published by Wordsong, an imprint of Boys Mills Press. Reprinted by permission.

"Ptarmigan," from *Polar Bear, Arctic Hare: Poems of the Frozen North* by Eileen Spinelli, illustrated by Eugenie Fernandes. Copyright © 2007 by Eileen Spinelli and Eugenie Fernandes. Published by Wordsong, an imprint of Boys Mills Press. Reprinted by permission.

"Caribou," from *Polar Bear, Arctic Hare: Poems of the Frozen North* by Eileen Spinelli, illustrated by Eugenie Fernandes. Copyright © 2007 by Eileen Spinelli and Eugenie Fernandes. Published by Wordsong, an imprint of Boys Mills Press. Reprinted by permission.

"Living Above Good Fortune," copyright © 2010 by Janet S. Wong. Used by permission of the author, who controls all rights.

"Walking Home from School," copyright © 2002 by Ann Whitford Paul. Used by permission of the author, who controls all rights.

"City Song," reprinted by permission of Michael Sampson.

Illustrations

61 Scott Angle

64 You Byun

122, 123 From *Amazing Faces,* illustration by Chris Soenpiet. Copyright © 2010 by Chris Soenpiet. Permission arranged with LEE & LOW BOOKS, Inc. New York, NY 10016. All rights not specifically granted herein are reserved.

124, 125 Glen Mullaly

Photographs

Photo locators denoted as follows: Top (T), Center (C), Bottom (B), Left (L), Right (R), Background (Bkgd)

27 (C) ©Ana Gram/Shutterstock, (CL) ©picsfive/Fotolia; 28 (C) ©Ana Gram/Shutterstock, (B) ©Monkey Business Images/Shutterstock; 29 ©Ana Gram/Shutterstock; 30 ©Trevor Clifford/Pearson Education Ltd; 31 ©Danny Smythe/Shutterstock; 32 (T) ©Tyler Olson/Shutterstock, (BL) ©auremar/Shutterstock; 33 ©Brand X Pictures/Getty Images; 34 ©JoeFox/Alamy; 35 ©Creatas/Thinkstock; 36 ©David Patrick Valera/Flickr/Getty Images; 38 ©lucielang/Fotolia; 39 ©Brand X Pictures/Getty Images; 62 ©Benelux/Corbis; 65 ©Purestock/Alamy; 66 (L) ©Tom Reichner/Shutterstock; 66 (R) ©Jack Cronkhite/Shutterstock; 67 ©Randy Yarbrough/Shutterstock; 68 ©ekler/Shutterstock; 69 ©Mira/Alamy; 70 ©Joel Bennett/CORBIS, ©Mira/Alamy; 71 (T)©Pat O'Hara/CORBIS, (R) ©Christie's Images/Corbis; 72 ©John Greim/age fotostock; 73 ©Horace Bristol/CORBIS; 74 ©CORBIS; 76 ©Associated Press; 105 ©prochasson frederic/Shutterstock; 106 ©Reed Kaestner/Corbis; 107 ©prochasson frederic/Shutterstock; 108 Mooch Images/Alamy; 109 Felix St Clair Renard/Getty; 110 Yann Layma/Getty ; 111 ©Dr. Gilbert H. Grosvenor/National Geographic Society/Corbis; 112 Michele Falzone/Alamy; 113 ©Mikhail Metzel/Associated Press; 114 ©Michael Newman/PhotoEdit; 115 Bill Bachman/Alamy; 116 John Stark/Alamy ; 117 John Henry Claude Wilson/Getty.